15 Minutes Alone with God

Emilie Barnes

HARVEST HOUSE PUBLISHERS
EUGENE, OREGON

Cover by Dugan Design Group, Bloomington, Minnesota

Cover photo Alison Miksch / Brand X Pictures / Jupiter Images

15 MINUTES ALONE WITH GOD
Copyright © 1994 by Harvest House Publishers
Eugene, Oregon 97402
www.harvesthousepublishers.com

Library of Congress Cataloging-in-Publication Data
Barnes, Emilie.
    15 minutes alone with God/Emilie Barnes.
        p. cm.
    ISBN 978-0-7369-5085-5 (Softcover)
    ISBN 978-0-7369-5086-2 (eBook)
    1. Women—Prayer—books and devotions—English. 2. Bible—Devotional literature. 3. Women—Religious life. 4. Women—Conduct of life. I. Title. II. Title: Fifteen minutes alone with God.
BV4844.B35   1994   94-6869
242 '8.643—dc20   CIP

Printed in the United States of America

17 18 19 20 / BP-KB / 9 8 7 6 5 4 3

Our grandchildren are a source of love and joy to me—

I dedicate this book to Christine, Chad, Bevan, Bradley Joe II, Weston, and those yet to come.

"Father God, thank You for all You do for our grandchildren. I pray that they will grow up to love You, serve You, honor and devour Your Word. I pray that they will be filled with knowledge, spiritual understanding, and wisdom, and that they might live a life worthy of You, Lord, and may please You from the top of their beautiful heads to the tip of their fingers to the bottom of their feet. May they walk in Your steps. In the name of Jesus, Amen."

Hugs,

Grammy Em

Fifteen Minutes
Alone with God

Traveling across America twenty-plus times a year speaking to women has given me a real heart for their hurting hearts. "No time, no time," they cry. "I have no time left for family, friends, housework, meals—let alone time to spend a quiet moment with God."

I've written this devotional book for every busy woman who wants to get in touch with her Lord and her life. Each quiet time is designed to take 15 minutes or less. That's not a huge commitment, but it's an important one. You'll spend some time in God's Word, and you'll find helps and direction for your everyday life.

Another unique feature is that you don't have to start at the beginning and go chapter by chapter. You can skip around if you would like. In the upper right-hand corner of each devotion, you will see three boxes. Put a checkmark in one of the boxes each time you read it. In this way, you can keep track of those devotions which have been read previously.

The 15-minute concept works! You just have to be willing to give it a try. Fifteen minutes a day for 21 days and you are on your way to devotions every day.

Allow God to hold your hand and lead you today to many quiet times with Him.

The only hope to the busy woman's cry is God Almighty Himself!

God the Father
God the Son
and
God the Holy Spirit

I love you all. May the Lord touch each quiet time with Him.

—Emilie

Power of Prayer

I got up early one morning and rushed into the day;
I had so much to accomplish that I didn't have time
to pray.

Problems just tumbled about me, and heavier came
each task.
"Why doesn't God help me?" I wondered. He
answered, "You didn't ask."

I wanted to see joy and beauty, but the day toiled
on, gray and bleak;
I wondered why God didn't show me. He said,
"But you didn't seek."

I tried to come into God's presence; I used all my
keys at the lock.
God gently and lovingly chided, "My child, you
didn't knock."

I woke up early this morning, and paused before
entering the day;
I had so much to accomplish that I had to take time
to pray.

—Author Unknown

Stand by Your God

Scripture Reading: Psalm 116:1-2

Key Verse: Psalm 116:2b
I will call on him as long as I live.

Consider the fruit that comes from spending time with your heavenly Father. In Galatians 5, Paul writes that "the fruit of the Spirit is love, joy, peace, patience, kindness, goodness, faithfulness, gentleness, self-control" (verses 22-23). Think about each item in that list. Which of us doesn't need a touch of God's love, patience, kindness, goodness, gentleness, and self-control in our life? Those are the things—as well as guidance, wisdom, hope, and a deeper knowledge of Him—that He wants to give to us as His children.

"But," you say, "who has time? My 'To Do' list is always longer than my day. I run from the time the alarm goes off in the morning until I fall into bed at night. How can I possibly find time to do one more thing? When could I find even a few minutes to read the Bible or pray?"

I answer your questions with a question: Are you doing what's *important* in your day—or only what is *urgent*?

People do what they want to do. All of us make choices, and when we don't make time for God in our day, when we don't make time for the most important relationship in our life, we are probably not making the best choices.

God greatly desires to spend time alone with you. After all, you are His child (John 1:12; Galatians 3:26). He created you,

---

7

He loves you, and He gave His only Son for your salvation. Your heavenly Father wants to know you, and He wants you to know Him. The Creator of the universe wants to meet with you alone daily. How can you say no to such an opportunity?

So make it your priority to spend time with God daily. There's not a single right time or one correct place. The only requirement for a right time with God is your willing heart. Your meeting time with God will vary according to the season of your life and the schedules you are juggling. Jesus often slipped away to be alone in prayer (Luke 5:16), but even His prayer times varied. He prayed in the morning and late at night, on a hill and in the upper room (Mark 1:35; Luke 22:41-45; Matthew 14:23; John 17).

I know people who spend hours commuting on the California freeways who use that time to be with God. I used to get up earlier than the rest of the family for a quiet time of reading the Scripture and praying. Now that the children are raised and the home is quiet, I find morning is still best for me, before the telephone starts to ring or I get involved in the day's schedule. And maybe I'm one of the oddballs, but I love getting to church early and having 10 or 15 minutes to open my Bible and think upon God's thoughts. Despite the distracting talk that is often going on around me, I use this block of time to prepare my heart for worship. (In fact, I believe if more members of the congregation devoted time to reading Scripture and praying for the service before the service, church would be more meaningful for every worshiper.)

Again, the times and places where we meet God will vary, but the fact that we meet alone with God each day should be a constant in our life. After all, God has made it clear that He is interested in us who are His children (1 Peter 5:7).

What should you do in your time alone with God? After you've read and meditated on God's Word for a while, spend some time with Him in prayer. Talk to Him as you would to your earthly parent or a special friend who loves you, desires the best for you, and wants to help you in every way possible.

Are you wondering what to talk to God about when you pray? Here are a few suggestions:

- *Praise* God for who He is, the Creator and Sustainer of the whole universe who is interested in each of us who are in His family (Psalm 150; Matthew 10:30).

- *Thank* God for all He has done for you...for all He is doing for you...and for all that He will do for you in the future (Philippians 4:6).

- *Confess* your sins. Tell God about the things you have done and said and thought for which you are sorry. He tells us in 1 John 1:9 that He is "faithful and righteous to forgive us our sins."

- *Pray* for your family...and for friends or neighbors who have needs, physical or spiritual. Ask God to work in the heart of someone you hope will come to know Jesus as Savior. Pray for our government officials, for your minister and church officers, for missionaries and other Christian servants (Philippians 2:4).

- *Pray, too, for yourself.* Ask for guidance for the day ahead. Ask God to help you do His will...and ask Him to arrange opportunities to serve Him throughout the day (Philippians 4:6).

Time with your heavenly Father is never wasted. If you spend time alone with God in the morning, you'll start your day refreshed and ready for whatever comes your way. If you spend time alone with Him in the evening, you'll go to sleep relaxed, resting in His care and ready for a new day to serve Him.

Remember, too, that you can talk to Him anytime, anywhere—in school, at work, on the freeway, at home—about anything. You don't have to make an appointment to ask Him for something you need or to thank Him for something you have received from Him. God is interested in everything that happens to you.

> *Father God, may I never forget to call on You in every situation. I want to call on You every day of my life and bring before You my adoration, confession, thanksgiving, and supplication. Thank You for being within the sound of my voice and only a thought's distance away. Amen.*

Thoughts for Action

❦ If you are not already spending time with God each day, decide today that you will give it a try for one month.

❦ Tell someone of your commitment and ask him or her to hold you accountable for that discipline.

Additional Scripture Reading

1 Peter 5:7
Matthew 6:6-13
1 Thessalonians 5:16-18

☑ ☐ ☐

A Prayer for All Seasons

Scripture Reading: Colossians 1:9-12

Key Verse: Colossians 1:9

> *Since the day we heard about you, we have not stopped praying for you and asking God to fill you with the knowledge of his will through all spiritual wisdom and understanding.*

Time has a way of defining true friends. I have discovered that passing years and growing distance are ineffective obstacles to the mutual love between my friends and me. Perhaps it is because of our common walk with the Lord that we can just pick up where we left off whenever we are together. And these are the dear ones I will spend eternity loving!

Of course, prayer is an important part of continuing that bond. Colossians 1:3-14 is an eloquent description of a Christian's prayer for her friends. Even though Paul had not even visited the Christians at Colosse (Colossians 1:7), his love for them through Christ was strong and ardent. (Taken from *The Women's Devotional Bible*. Copyright © 1990 by The Zondervan Corporation. Used by permission of Zondervan Publishing House.)

As we spend time with God, we open ourselves to His work in our hearts and in our lives. Then, as we see Him working, we will want to know Him even more. We will want our prayer life to be all that it can be. What does that mean? How should we be praying?

In the Scripture, we find many models of prayer, and probably foremost is the Lord's Prayer (Matthew 6:9-13). This wonderful example of a prayer includes important elements of prayer. We find words of adoration, of submission to God's will, of petition, and in closing, of praise. We can learn much from the model our Lord gave when His disciples said, "Teach us to pray" (Luke 11:1).

As meaningful as the Lord's Prayer is to me, I have also found Colossians 1:9-12 to be a powerful guide in my prayer life. If you aren't in the habit of praying or if you want to renew your time with God, I challenge you to read this passage of Scripture every day for 30 days. Look at it in small pieces, dwell on its message each day, take action upon what it says, and you'll become a new person.

Read today's Scripture passage again and think about what a wonderful prayer it is for you to pray for your friend. Knowing that a friend is praying for me is a real source of encouragement and support. If you aren't praying for your friends daily, let me suggest that Colossians 1:9-12 be your model. Look at what you'll be asking God:

- That your friend will have the spiritual wisdom and understanding she needs to know God's will.

- That she will "walk in a manner worthy of the Lord, to please him, in all respects" (verse 10).

- That your friend will be bearing "fruit in all good work and increasing in the knowledge of God" (verse 10).

- That she will be "strengthened with all power...for the attaining of all steadfastness and patience" (verse 11).

You would then end your prayer by joyously giving thanks to God for all that He has given you—your friend being one of those gifts (verse 12).

Did you hear those words? What an armor of protection and growth you can give your friend with a prayer like that! With these powerful words and the Lord at her side, your friend will be able to deal with the challenges she faces. I also encourage you to tell your friend that you are praying for her each day, and if she is receptive, tell her the specifics of your prayers for her. Let me assure you that it is a real comfort to have a friend praying for me, asking God to give me wisdom and understanding, to enable me to honor Him in all I do, to help me bear fruit for His kingdom, and to grant me strength, steadfastness, and patience.

Know, too, that these verses from Colossians are a good model for your prayers for your husband, other members of your family, your neighbors, and yourself. After all, all of God's people need to know His will, honor Him in everything they do, grow in the knowledge of the Lord, and be strong, steadfast, and patient as we serve Him.

Thoughts for Actions

❦ In your journal, write down the names of one to three friends that you want to pray for each day. Under each name list several specific areas which you want to pray for them.

❦ Read Colossians 1:9-12 for 30 straight days. Think specifically of the friends you listed in your journal.

Additional Scripture Reading

Ephesians 3:14-19   Philemon 4-7

*Prayer pushes the light and hope
into little dark corners of your life.*

☑ ❏ ❏

I Didn't Believe It

Scripture Reading: John 6:35-40

Key Verse: John 6:40

> For my Father's will is that everyone who looks to the Son and believes in him shall have eternal life, and I will raise him up at the last day.

Bob and I arrived to our hotel late after flying from California to Hartford, Connecticut. It was our first holiday seminar for the season, and the church put us up at a beautiful Ramada Inn. We were anxious to see the turning of the leaves for the first time, and they were at their peak in early October.

We registered at the hotel, went directly to our room, took a hot bath, and crawled into bed. It felt so good after the waits, plane layovers, airport terminal delays, crowded cramped seating, and heavy luggage. We both fell into a much-needed sleep about 9:30 P.M.

Two and a half hours later we were wakened by what we thought was a smoke alarm. My Bob rolled to the phone to call the front desk while I peeked out the peephole in the door. I couldn't see any smoke, but Bob was not getting an answer from the front desk. He let the phone ring and ring as the alarm got stronger and louder. I peeked out the peephole again, only to see a man running down the hall pulling his pants and jacket on. "Bob, it's a fire!" I yelled. "People are evacuating the building."

Bob quickly hung up, and we put some clothes on—not much and I'm not sure what. We grabbed our briefcases and swiftly left the room. By now many other guests were doing the same. The alarm was still blasting, and we heard the sirens of the fire trucks headed for the hotel. As we walked toward the stairs to hurry down six flights, we ran into people pushing through to get ahead. One lady kept yelling, "Hurry, Ruth! Hurry, Ruth!" as she passed us. Poor Ruth! Her legs just couldn't move as fast as the others. We finally made it out into the very chilly, 34° midnight air. The whole hotel had been evacuated onto the street, and firefighters were all over—only to find it was a false alarm. People calmly headed back to their rooms.

As we got off the elevator on our floor, a little lady peeped out her door in her nighty and asked, "Was it a fire?"

"False alarm," we answered.

"Well, I didn't believe it anyway."

Crawling back into bed Bob and I both thought how that woman's words echoed the sentiment of so many at Jesus' first coming. "I didn't believe it anyway." How many had heard the message, saw the messenger Jesus, saw His miracles—and still didn't believe?

Today the message is clear: Jesus is here. The Bible tells us the truth, the life, the love, and the message of salvation. Today's Scripture reading tells us to believe and we will receive eternal life. However, it's as true today as it was 2000 years ago—many say, "I didn't believe it." One day we will find that His Word is truth, and for some it will be too late.

Father God, never let me get to the point of unbelief. I have seen hardened hearts, and I don't want that to be me. I have found You to be believable in the past—and I know You will be in the future, too. Amen.

Thoughts for Action

❦ Share with a friend how you came to believe in Christ.

❦ Begin today to read the Bible, believing that it is God's inspired Word.

❦ I conclude my holiday seminar with this poem. As a thought for action, read it and expect a tear or two. Let your heart be touched.

'Twas the Night Before Jesus Came

'Twas the night before Jesus came and all through the house
Not a creature was praying, not one in the house.
Their Bibles were lain on the shelf without care
In hopes that Jesus would not come there.

The children were dressing to crawl into bed,
Not once ever kneeling or bowing a head.
And Mom in her rocker and baby on her lap
Was watching the Late Show while I took a nap.

When out of the East there arose such a clatter,
I sprang to my feet to see what was the matter.
Away to the window I flew like a flash
Tore open the shutters and threw up the sash!

When what to my wondering eyes should appear
But angels proclaiming that Jesus was here.
With a light like the sun sending forth a bright ray
I knew in a moment this must be THE DAY!

The light of His face made me cover my head.
It was Jesus! Returning just like He had said.
And though I possessed worldly wisdom and wealth,
I cried when I saw Him in spite of myself.
In the Book of Life which He held in His hand,

Was written the name of every saved man.
He spoke not a word as He searched for my name;
When He said, "It's not here," my head hung in shame.

The people whose names had been written with love
He gathered to take to His Father above.
With those who were ready He rose without a sound
While all the rest were left standing around.

I fell to my knees, but it was too late;
I had waited too long and thus sealed my fate.
I stood and I cried as they rose out of sight;
Oh, if only I had been ready tonight.

In the words of this poem the meaning is clear;
The coming of Jesus is drawing near.
There's only one life and when comes the last call
We'll find that the Bible was true after all![1]

Additional Scripture Reading

2 Timothy 3:16   Acts 13:38-39

Be Content
in Everything

Scripture Reading: 1 Timothy 6:1-10

Key Verse: 1 Timothy 6:6
> But godliness with contentment is great gain.

One of the Barnes' famous sayings is, "If you're not happy with what you have, you'll never be satisfied with what you want." I meet so many people who are always looking to the future—the next paycheck, the next home, the next church, the next month, the next school, and, in some cases, the next marriage partner. We are a country characterized by discontent. Do you find yourself being drawn into this mindset?

Recently I was visiting our newest grandchild, Bradley Joe Barnes II. As I was holding him, rubbing my hands through his hair, tracing the shape of his toes and fingers, my mind went to thinking about what he was going to be as he grew to manhood. Was he going to have good grades and go to college? Would he be a fireman, a pastor, a teacher, a coach, a salesman? Suddenly I realized that I was thinking about *what* he could be rather than focusing my thoughts and prayers on *who* he would be.

In today's culture we are all drawn away from spiritual pursuits to putting our hope into wealth (1 Timothy 6:17) and to building our lives around ways to accomplish this ambition. As I sat there in Bradley Joe's room, I began praying that all of his extended family might teach him higher values than money, career, and fame. Not that these are evil, but the value we place on them can lead to our downfall (1 Timothy 6:9).

In today's passage Paul states, "Godliness with contentment is great gain" (1 Timothy 6:6). When we find ourselves looking to the future because we aren't content with today, may God give us a peace of mind that lets us rest where He has placed us. Be content in today!

> *Father God, You know that my heart's desire is to be content in whatever state I'm in. I want to be like Paul in that regard. You have given me so much and I want to graciously thank You for those blessings. Amen.*

Thoughts for Action

❦ Instead of being preoccupied with your station in life, start praising God for where you are.

❦ Pray to God asking Him to reveal to you what you are to learn in your present situation.

❦ Write a letter to God thanking Him for all your blessings. Name them individually.

Additional Scripture Reading

1 Timothy 6:11-21   Proverbs 22:1-2
Mark 10:17-25

☑ ❑ ❑

What a Friend!

Scripture Reading: 2 Timothy 1:16-18
Key Verse: 2 Timothy 1:18b
> You know very well in how many ways he helped me
> in Ephesus.

Oh, how our heart yearns to have friends! In today's
Scripture reading we find the ways in which Onesiphorus
helped Paul: 1) He often refreshed him, 2) he was not
ashamed of Paul's chains, and 3) he searched hard for Paul
until he found him.

I'd like to share a story with you about another friendship:

> Damon was sentenced to die on a certain day, and
> sought permission of Dionysius of Syracuse to visit his
> family in the interim. It was granted, on condition of
> securing a hostage for himself. Pythias heard of it, and vol-
> unteered to stand in his friend's place. The king visited
> him in prison, and conversed with him about the motive
> of his conduct; affirming his disbelief in the influence of
> friendship. Pythias expressed his wish to die that his
> friend's honor might be vindicated. He prayed the gods to
> delay the return of Damon till after his own execution in
> his stead.

> The fatal day arrived. Dionysius sat on a moving
> throne, drawn by six white horses. Pythias mounted the

scaffold, and calmly addressed the spectators: "My prayer is heard: the gods are propitious; for the winds have been contrary till yesterday. Damon could not come; he could not conquer impossibilities; he will be here tomorrow, and the blood which is shed today shall have ransomed the life of my friend. Oh! could I erase from your bosoms every mean suspicion of the honor of Damon, I should go to my death as I would to my bridal. My friend will be found noble, his truth unimpeachable; he will speedily prove it; he is now on his way, accusing himself, the adverse elements, and the gods: but I haste to prevent his speed. Executioner, do your office."

As he closed, a voice in the distance cried, "Stop the execution!" which was repeated by the whole assembly. A man rode up at full speed, mounted the scaffold, and embraced Pythias, crying, "You are safe, my beloved friend! I now have nothing but death to suffer, and am delivered from reproaches for having endangered a life so much dearer than my own."

Pythias replied, "Fatal haste, cruel impatience! What envious powers have wrought impossibilities in your favor? But I will not be wholly disappointed. Since I cannot die to save, I will not survive you."

The king heard, and was moved to tears. Ascending the scaffold he cried, "Live, live, ye incomparable pair! Ye have borne unquestionable testimony to the existence of virtue; and that virtue equally evinces the existence of a God to reward it. Live happy, live renowned, and oh! form me by your precepts, as ye have invited me by your example, to be worthy of the participation of so sacred a friendship."

If heathenism had such friendships, what may be expected of Christianity?[2]

If the world is to pay attention to us as Christians and to our lifestyle, we must reflect true friendship with those people we contact each day.

> *Father God, thank You for my many friends who stand beside me in all situations. They are always there when I need them to listen, laugh, and cry. They are so special to my life. May they realize what their friendship means to me. Amen.*

Thoughts for Action

❦ Go out today and refreshen someone's life through a kind word or action.

❦ Ask the Lord to give you a heart that is not ashamed of another person's "chains"—those things that put him or her in a different status of life than your own.

❦ Seek out a friend you haven't seen for a while.

Additional Scripture Reading

Proverbs 18:24   Luke 10:33-34
Proverbs 27:17

One Day at a Time

Scripture Reading: Zechariah 4:1-7

Key Verse: Zechariah 4:6b
> *"Not by might nor by power, but by my Spirit," says the LORD Almighty.*

Dear Mrs. Barnes:

I've just finished reading your book *Survival for Busy Women*. I feel that it helped me a good bit. It's very easy for me to get down because of my daily schedule. I know you're a very busy woman, but if you have a few minutes to look at my average daily schedule and offer any helpful ideas about how to organize my day better so I would have more time to spend with my husband and six-year-old son, I would greatly appreciate it.

5:45-6:50 A.M.	Get ready for work.
6:50-7:15	Fix a quick bite of breakfast for my little boy. Pack his snack and my lunch for the day.
7:20	Leave home to take my son to school. I go on to work.
8:00	Get to work. (At work I'm able to do all of my personal paperwork, read my Bible, etc.)

5:00 P.M.	Get off work.
5:20	Pick up my son.
5:35	Get home. (I get home at this time if I do nothing else but go straight home.)
5:35-6:30	Help my son with his homework. Do minor housework.
6:45-8:00	Load up my son's bike to go down to the track so I can walk for one hour.
8:00	Fix a bite of supper while my son takes his shower and gets ready for bed. Between 8 and 9 we eat.
9:00	Get my son into bed. I need to go to bed also, but I'm usually trying to wash or fold clothes or clean up the kitchen. Sometimes it's 11 before I go to bed.

I never do any "housecleaning" during the week, and I hardly vacuum the floors on the weekend. Most of the time I just can't stand doing major housecleaning on my only day off (besides Sunday, of course, but I'm not cleaning house on Sunday—that day is filled with church and family).

With a schedule like this, when do I have time to spend with my husband or my child?

This woman leads an active life! I imagine she often feels like a juggler in a circus. Sound familiar to you? Many of us are overwhelmed by the pressures and responsibilities we face, yet we still keep taking on more and more. We have not learned to say "No" to good things and save our "Yeses" for the best.

Are there some good things we are doing which we should say no to? We are not superwomen. The secular world has led us down the path of lies which says, "We can do it all. We can have it all." Very few of us are that capable. We must learn to major on the major issues of life and not get sidetracked on the minors that drain us of all the creativity, energy, and productivity God has given us.

A good way to major on the major issues is to learn to live one day at a time. Go to the Lord each day and seek His guidance and wisdom for today—not tomorrow, not next week, not next year, but today. There is great value in doing a "TO DO" list each day as well. On a pad of paper list only those things that need to be done today, not tomorrow or next week, but just today. After a few days of making lists, you will find yourself having to rank your activities by priority, certain things being more important than others. Concentrate on the most important activity first and let the least important items settle to the end of the day. (Some of these will even drop off the page, because of their low priority.) You will be amazed at how much you will accomplish when you do this one project—a TO DO list.

At night as you crawl into bed, look at your list, smile, and thank God for helping you stay on schedule. Utter a prayer of thanksgiving that expresses your appreciation for God giving you the power to say no to "minor" requests.

Father God, I pray for my schedules. I ask for
wise discernment in order to gain control of my life.
Give me the courage to say "no" to the time wasters
and say "yes" to the things that have eternal value.
Amen.

Thoughts for Action

❧ Make tomorrow's TO DO list before you go to bed tonight.

❧ Share your list with the Lord and ask Him to help you honor this list.

❧ Check off (✔) each item as you complete your activity.

❧ Reward yourself at the end of the day. (However, no fat grams are allowed!)

❧ It takes 21 days to establish a new habit.

❧ Do it again tomorrow.

Additional Scripture Reading

Ecclesiastes 2:17-26   Philippians 3:12-14

Becoming as Gold

Scripture Reading: Job 23:1-12

Key Verse: Job 23:10
> But he knows the way that I take when he has tested me, I will come forth as gold.

When pain comes into our lives it's so easy to ask "Why, Lord? Why, Lord, do the righteous suffer?"

If there ever was a man who loved and obeyed God, it was Job. Yet his testing was very dramatic and ever so painful. Today all we have to do is pick up a newspaper in any part of the world and we can read of tragedy touching the just and the unjust.

Our friends Glen and Marilyn Heavilin have lost three sons prematurely: one to crib death, one twin, Ethan, to pneumonia as an infant, then the second twin, Nathan, was killed as a teenager by a drunk driver. Were Glen and Marilyn tested? You bet. Yet did they come forth as gold? You bet! Today they use their experiences to glorify the name of the Lord.

Marilyn has written five books. Her first, *Roses in December*,[3] tells the story of their great loss. Marilyn has had the opportunity to speak all over the country in high school auditoriums filled with teenagers. There she shares her story and has the platform to talk about life and death, chemical dependency, and God Himself.

Did God know what He was doing when He chose the Heavilins? You bet. They have come forth as gold fired in the heat of life and polished to shine for Him. Is their pain gone? Never. Can they go forth to minister? Absolutely. They have been very active in a group called "Compassionate Friends" which supports families who have experienced the death of a child. I thank God for Christians like the Heavilins. God knew the way they would take when tragedy came into their lives.

Everyone has experienced some kind of tragedy. How we handle these events when they happen is key. Today there are so many wonderful support groups available in churches and the local communities.

I grew up with a violent, alcoholic father. I had no place to go and no one to talk to, so I stuffed my pain. Now there are several groups to help people who find themselves in situations like mine.

A church in Southern California has a large group that meets weekly and has become like a church within a church for those who are chemically dependent and their families. Lives have changed as they pray for each other, support each other, and cry together. Many are coming forth as gold.

Bob and I visited a church in Memphis, Tennessee, which had a support group for homosexuals. Because of this church's outreach, many were coming out of the gay lifestyle and coming forth as gold.

Whatever your test is today, please know that others have experienced and are experiencing your pain. Don't go through the testing alone. Contact the local church and find another with whom you can share and cry. You, too, can and will come forth as gold.

Jesus knows and has also experienced our pain. He is always with us to help us get through the tough times in life. Trust Him now. It's all part of the coming forth as gold that Job talks about.

Father God, it is hard to desire testing in order to be more Christlike. However, I know from experience that we rarely grow in good times. It's the intense heat that makes us pure. May I be gold and not wood, hay, or stubble. Amen.

Thoughts for Action

❦ Write down in your journal what pain and/or test you are experiencing today.

❦ Take a step to help yourself work toward becoming as gold.

❦ Write a letter to God about how you feel.

❦ Get involved in a support group.

Additional Scripture Reading

Psalm 66:10	2 Corinthians 4:7-9
Psalm 51:10	

We must always
remember that God
has given to every soul
the responsibility of
deciding what its
character and destiny
shall be.

—Charles Jefferson

A House Divided

Scripture Reading: Mark 3:24-27

Key Verse: Mark 3:5
> *If a house is divided against itself, that house cannot stand.*

"A house divided against itself cannot stand," Abraham Lincoln said in his acceptance speech of his nomination for the United States Senate. "Either the opponents of slavery will arrest the further spread of it and place it where the public mind shall rest in the belief that it is in the course of ultimate extinction, or its advocates will push it forward, till it shall become alike lawful in all the states, old as well as new—north as well as south."

Lincoln's pursuit of the equality of peoples eventually brought his defeat in the Senate election. Lincoln responded to his downfall philosophically: "...and though I now sink out of view and shall be forgotten, I believe I have made some marks which will tell for the cause of civil liberty long after I am gone." Lincoln certainly didn't "sink out of view"! He left marks not only upon our country but on the whole world. His gift to the United States was to heal those hurts that wanted to divide us, to bring together those who had been at war.

Many of our families are divided and need to be healed and brought together. I had two aunts (they were sisters) who hadn't spoken to each other for 10 years because of some insignificant verbal disagreement. They behaved like little children with small hurts who could not let their souls confess their error. As I saw my aunts get older without sharing their later years in harmony, I decided that I was going to be the peacemaker, even though I was 30-plus years younger than they were. I was able to arrange a family gathering where both attended. After a short time together in this setting, they began to open up and talk to each other. By the end of the evening they had made amends. Because of this reuniting, they were able to enjoy the last 15 years of their lives together as sisters.

Maybe you have division in your family. As today's Scripture reading states, "If a kingdom is divided against itself, that kingdom cannot stand." If we stay divided we know what the outcome will be—collapse of the family unit. You become the healer of your divided home. It will take much prayer, patience, and conviction, but in the end you'll discover that a united house has many blessings.

> By wisdom a house is built, and through understanding it is established; through knowledge its rooms are filled with rare and beautiful treasures (Proverbs 24:3-4).

You be the one to restore your house with a rare and beautiful spirit.

> *Father God, may I be a healer in my family. May my spirit be one that unifies rather than divides. Show me any traits that I might have that need change. I thank You for being here when I need You. Thank You for Your continuing love and Your sweet spirit. Amen.*

Thoughts for Action

- Pray about and identify one person in your family who needs to be reunited with your family.

- Seek your spouse's support in this prayer need.

- Establish a plan on how to reunite this family member with the family.

- Step out and risk rejection.

Additional Scripture Reading

Matthew 12:25   Luke 11:17-22

Make Me a Blessing

Scripture Reading: Song of Songs 2:8-13

Key Verse: Song of Songs 2:12a

> *Flowers appear on the earth; the season of singing has come.*

My Bob loves to drive from Riverside to San Diego each spring after it rains. Within a few days after these soft rains, the banks of the freeway are covered with the delicately waving state flower—the golden poppy. Truly the "Golden State" is golden. What a beautiful array of God's creation in flower form.

For a few years we had severe drought in California and the flowers were thinly populated. But now rain has returned and we are lavishly blessed with the golden poppy again. Our key verse for today states, "Flowers appear on the earth; the season of singing has come." All fall and winter the seeds lay dormant in the ground, and then the rains come and turn these seeds into a song.

Our lives are like that at times. We may lie sleeping—forgotten, we think. Then something happens that makes us come forward, take a look at the sun, and decide we are going to be a blessing to someone today. May today be that day when we reach out, near or far, and bless someone.

I watched the golden poppies spill

34

Like liquid gold across the hill
As petals wilted one by one
And faded with the summer sun.
The plants did not reseed themselves
To golden-glow the hillside shelves;
The rains that washed the mountain's face
Transplanted them some other place.
But when I walk their trail I find
My feet are light; my heart gold-lined—
Knowing, though they left no chart,
They gladden someone else's heart.[4]

Thoughts for Action

- Reach out and be a blessing to someone today.

- Telephone, write a letter, drop a note, send a gift—be that golden poppy in someone's life.

- Don't put any expectations on your actions. Act out of pure love.

- Record a blessing to someone on an audio cassette tape and mail it to them.

Additional Scripture Reading

    Hebrews 10:24-25   Romans 15:29
    Ephesians 5:1

In His Steps

Scripture Reading: 1 Peter 2:13-25

Key Verse: 1 Peter 2:21

> *To this you were called, because Christ suffered for you, leaving you an example, that you should follow in his steps.*

———— ❦ ————

Many years ago I read a book entitled *In His Steps*. It was the story of a man who for a period of time attempted to walk in the steps of Jesus. Everything he said, everywhere he went, all decisions he made were done as if he were Jesus. As you can imagine, it was just about impossible. However, the experience changed this man's life forever.

We are not Jesus—nor will we ever be. Yet Jesus left us with His example of a godly life. As we walk through life on earth we will experience daily situations that will reveal our character. Jesus gives us the example of kindness and gentleness. He was full of sympathy and affection, and always loved with mercy.

Jesus said, "Beloved, I understand your pain, your grief, the tragedy of friends who betray you. I know you live in a world where others have sickness and sin you can do nothing about. I care, and I can help you. I can cleanse you and heal you today." As the Lord lives in you, He will form you into the beautiful, marvelous image of God according to your own uniqueness.

No we can't be Jesus. But we can develop a teachable spirit. We can love Him and desire Him in our hearts with all our soul, mind, and strength. We will then find ourselves transformed into a giving, loving spirit with the joy of Jesus in our hearts. Our character will then reveal the likeness of Jesus. Our spirits will help the helpless, pray for the sick, feed and clothe the homeless, and support those whom God lifts up to be missionaries where we can't go.

May we walk in His steps as we follow His call to us today.

Father God, oh You know how I want to be like
You. The deepest part of my heart and soul aches for
Your wisdom. May today be a special day for new
revelation. Amen.

Thoughts for Action

- Ask yourself, "Are the qualities of Jesus evident in my life?"

- How can you follow in His steps today? List at least one way.

Additional Scripture Reading

Ephesians 2:6-7   John 15:12

The Minimum Daily Adult Requirement

Scripture Reading: Ephesians 2:4-9

Key Verse: Ephesians 2:8-9

> For it is by grace you have been saved, through faith—and this not from yourselves, it is the gift of God—not by works, so that no one can boast.

A couple of years ago I had a young college student ask me, "How much beer can I drink as a Christian?" Others have asked:

- How long should I read my Bible each day?
- How long should I pray each day?
- How much money do I have to give to the church?
- Do I have to sing in the choir to be a good Christian?
- How many times a week must I be in church?
- Do I have to _____, _____, _____?

On and on we go. We all want to know what the "minimum daily adult requirement" is for being a Christian. What do we *really* have to do, day-by-day, to get by?

Sue Gregg and I have written a lot of cookbooks dealing with God-given principles for a balanced lifestyle regarding food. The American consumer is very sophisticated when it comes to reading labels. Some even have small calculators with them as they stroll the aisle with shopping carts under tow. They can tell you unit costs, what kind of sugar is being used, what the derivative of the fat content is, how many calories, how much sodium, what is the nutritional information per serving, and yes, even the percentages of the minimum daily adult requirement.

If we want to know about the daily requirements in regard to our food, should we not also be concerned about this in our Christian walk? Of course! It only makes sense that we would definitely want to know how long Christians pray, how long they read their Bible, how much money they should put in the offering plate, how many church activities they participate in each week, etc.

Paul addresses these very basic questions in Ephesians. He very clearly states, "For it is by grace you have been saved, through faith—and this not from yourselves, it is the gift of God—not by works, so that no one can boast" (verses 8-9). Christ has freed us from this bondage of minimum daily adult requirements! It is not of works, but of grace.

You might ask, "Do I do nothing as a Christian? Aren't there some requirements?" The Scriptures challenge us to be like Christ. If I am to grow as unto the Lord, I need to study to see what He did and how He did it. For example,

- I find Him studying the law.
- I see Him meeting with other believers.
- I see Him praying regularly.
- I see Him serving others around Him in need.
- I see Him giving to those in need.

<u>Christ did not do them because He was *told* to do them.
He did them because He *wanted* to do them.</u>
Seek from the Holy Spirit what your minimum daily adult
requirement is. It is different for every one of us.

> *Father God, help me not to worry about how
> long or how often. Put a strong desire in my soul to
> spend time with You today in prayer and study. Let
> time stand still and let me forget all about my watch
> and schedule. Amen.*

Thoughts for Action

- 𝕏 List in your journal the things you are doing because you think they are required of you as a Christian.

- 𝕏 Cross off the things you don't want to do.

- 𝕏 Why are you still doing those things that are left? Cross some more off the list.

- 𝕏 Now list only those activities that you feel you want to do in order to grow unto the Lord. You may very well have the same list, but the items are listed because you want to do them rather than someone telling you to do them. Simply stated, this is grace and not law.

Additional Scripture Reading

1 Corinthians 1:4-8   Ephesians 6:5-8
2 Timothy 1:8-10

☑ ❑ ❑

The Whys of Life

Scripture Reading: Ecclesiastes 7:13-18

Key Verse: Ecclesiastes 7:16
> Do not be overrighteous, neither be overwise—why destroy yourself?

───── ❧ ─────

You have to know that fame is fleeting, and I know—I always had my parents to refresh my memory.

No matter how important you think you are, they taught me, you're a mere nothing in the passage of time. Once you reach a certain level in a material way, what more can you do? You can't eat more than three meals a day; you'll kill yourself. You can't wear two suits, one over the other. You might now have three cars in your garage—but six! Oh, you can indulge yourself, but only to a point.

One way to make sure fame doesn't change you is to keep in mind that you're allotted only so much time on this earth—and neither money nor celebrity will buy you a couple of extra days. Although I do have a rich friend in New York who says, "What do you mean I can't take it with me? I've already made out traveler's checks and sent them ahead."

Life is so complicated that it's hard for anyone, especially kids, to figure out what their purpose is in life, and
to whom they're accountable. Of course, we should all be
accountable to God throughout our lives—and live our
lives that way every day, not just on our deathbeds begging
for forgiveness.

A lot of people don't believe in God because they
can't see Him. I'm not a Doubting Thomas, though. I truly
believe. When we were kids, our Sunday school teachers
used to address this question by telling us: "You can't see
electricity either, but it's there. Just stick your hand in the
socket now and then to remind yourself." I've never seen
an ozone layer or carbon monoxide or an AIDS virus, but
they're out there somewhere.[5]

Lee Iacocca has learned a very valuable lesson in life, and
that is balance and proper prospective toward wealth and
fame. The wise man will live life in obedience to God, recognizing that God will eventually judge all men.

In today's Scripture reading we see that God brings both
prosperity and adversity into our lives for His sovereign purpose without always revealing His plan. Our minds do not
have the horsepower to think as God does. By faith we must
rely on His words to do what He says He will do. A long time
ago Bob and I claimed 2 Timothy 3:16-17 as one of our important verses of Scripture:

> All Scripture is God-breathed and is useful
> for teaching, rebuking, correcting and training in
> righteousness, so that the man of God may be
> thoroughly equipped for every good work.

Are you being equipped to handle life: birth, death, fame,
divorce, fortune, bankruptcy, health, sickness? When we're
young we often think we know all the answers of life. But as
we get older we begin to realize that we fit into a master plan
that can't always be explained.

Have you ever asked the question, "Why?" Of course you have. We all have. That is the mystery question of life. Solomon realized that God has a sovereign purpose, and that He doesn't always reveal to us the key to His plan.

> *Father God, humble my spirit so that I might be open to new truths today that I might better understand the whys of life (the big and the small). You know that I want to expand my mind to be more like You! Amen.*

Thoughts for Action

❦ In your journal list several of your "why" questions. Realize that you will not always know the answer to these whys.

❦ Turn these questions over to God in prayer and give them up to Him. Someday you will realize how these whys fit into His sovereign plans.

❦ Thank God, also, for all the questions you have answers for.

Additional Scripture Reading

Ecclesiastes 3:1-8   Ecclesiastes 3:14
Ecclesiastes 9:1

☑ ☐ ☐

Is Your Mate Looking Upward?

Scripture Reading: Genesis 2:18-23

Key Verse: Genesis 2:18
> *It is not good for the man to be alone. I will make a helper suitable for him.*

A pastor meeting an irreligious lady whose husband was trying to serve God addressed her thus: "Madam, I think your husband is looking upwards, making some effort to rise above the world towards God and heaven. You must not let him try alone. Whenever I see the husband struggling alone in such efforts, it makes me think of a dove endeavoring to fly upwards while it has one broken wing. It leaps and flutters, and perhaps rises a little way; and then it becomes wearied, and drops back again to the ground. If both wings cooperate, then it mounts easily."

This principle is one of the great principles of marriage. What a difference it would make if more women would uphold their husbands as they attempt to rise above the world towards God and heaven! In his letter to Titus, the apostle Paul gives some excellent exaltations to women. He writes:

> ...train the younger women to love their
> husbands and children, to be self-controlled and

pure, to be busy at home, to be kind, and to be subject to their husbands, so that no one will malign the word of God (Titus 2:4-5).

Oh, how we need to teach our women:

- to love their husbands and children.
- to be self-controlled.
- to be pure.
- to be busy at home.
- to be kind.
- to be subject to their husbands.

These traits are so contrary to what the world is attempting to teach you. Unfortunately the world's ways seem to be winning, so how about stepping forward and trying God's ways? I am not a strong supporter of "formulas that work," but these six characteristics will definitely help your husband reach up unto God.

Thoughts for Action

❦ Do something to lift your husband heavenward.

❦ Concentrate on one of the six principles from the Titus list.

❦ Tell your husband how much you love him.

Additional Scripture Reading

1 Peter 3:1-7   Ephesians 5:21-28

☑ ☐ ☐

His Outstretched Hand

Scripture Reading: Isaiah 53:3-10

Key Verse: Isaiah 53:3a

He was despised and rejected by men, a man of sorrows and familiar with suffering.

The pain of rejection can hurt so bad that you think you want to die. We all have experienced it from time to time, probably from someone we cared about very deeply—a parent, husband, child, friend, brother or sister, or possibly all the above.

What great pain this can cause, and yet we can overcome the pain of rejection. Yes, there is life after rejection.

Jesus Himself experienced rejection. If anyone knows this pain, it's Jesus. His own people who He came to save and teach were the very ones who nailed Him to the cross: "He came to that which was his own, but his own did not receive him" (John 1:11).

My Jewish family wanted me to marry within my own faith. Yet when I was 16, my Bob introduced me to Christ. Within a few months Bob and I were engaged, and eight months later we were married. My very own family, those I loved, rejected me for my stand with Jesus and my stand to marry the Christian young man I loved.

God honored my heart and my faithfulness to Him. My family grew to adore my Bob as I do, and our family was restored.

It didn't happen all at once, but in His time, one by one, hearts were softened and attitudes changed. The pain in my heart was great, but little by little His mighty strength took over and peace filled my heart. I hung in and loved my family when it was difficult to love the attitudes and mockery thrown at me. I'm grateful today I trusted Jesus.

Isaiah prophesied that Messiah would be despised and rejected of men, yet this foreknowledge did not make the experience any less painful for Jesus. And to make it even worse, Jesus felt rejected by His own Father. When Jesus bore the sins of the world He felt deep, deep pain. He cried out, "My God, my God, why have you forsaken me?" (Matthew 27:46).

Yet in the middle of all this rejection, Jesus never abandoned the mission that God had given to Him. He never fought back against the ones who rejected Him. How did He respond? With love—love even for those who crucified Him.

Do you think the Lord knows how you feel? You bet! And the Lord Jesus offers you His strength. The Bible says that He sympathizes with our weakness and He offers His grace for our time of need. When Jesus suffered on the cross, He bore our penalty for us. He paid the price for our sins. Then He gave us a promise: "Never will I leave you; never will I forsake you" (Hebrews 13:5). No matter what happens, God will never reject you. You will never be alone again. You may be rejected by others, but remember God Almighty will always be there to comfort you. His hand is stretched out to you. All you need to do is place your hands in His. Allow His strength to empower you today.

> *Father God, You know rejection far better than I do. I ask You to touch me when I'm rejected (or when I feel rejected) and ease that pain. Please make me sensitive to the times when I reject people. You know that I don't want to hurt others' feelings. Protect my words, body language, and attitude, that they may heal and not reject. Amen.*

Thoughts for Action

 Don't dwell on your pain but place it in Jesus' hands today.

Additional Scripture Reading

Philippians 4:13   Hebrews 4:15-16
2 Corinthians 1:3   John 1:1-5

☑ ❑ ❑

Your True Motivation

Scripture Reading: Matthew 19:27–20:16

Key Verse: Matthew 19:29

> And everyone who has left houses or brothers or sisters or father or mother or children or fields for my sake will receive a hundred times as much and will inherit eternal life.

Throughout my life I have asked myself over and over, why do I serve? What is my motivation for speaking, writing, giving financially to the church, being a mother, giving freely to my husband and to my extended family?

In today's passage Peter asks Jesus, "What then will there be for us?" Have you ever caught yourself asking this very basic question? I know I have. When Bob was in business, he would share with me the reaction from different employees when he would tell them about a promotion they were going to receive. Most would ask:

- How much more money will I make?

- Any increase in health insurance, vacations, bonuses, retirement, etc?

In the verses you read, Jesus answers Peter's very basic question, giving us three important principles for our daily living:

- Whatever we give up we will receive a hundred times as much.

- We will inherit eternal life.

- Many who are first will be last, and many who are last will be first.

<u>Many times in our religious life we think God will punish us if we don't serve Him rather than being truly motivated by a pure desire to serve Him.</u>

My daily prayer is for God to reveal to me what my true motivation is in serving Him. In Psalm 139:1 David states, "O Lord, you have searched me and you know me." I truly yearn to know me as God knows me.

Can I accept from God the promises He has given me in today's beautiful reading? Do I honestly accept by faith what God has so graciously given to us, a hundredfold return for all we have given up *and* eternal life because of our acceptance of Jesus?

As I look around to see what God has so graciously given to me, I am amazed and blessed at His generosity. As the old church hymn says, "Count your blessings, name them one by one." Name a few:

- I know Jesus face-to-face

- salvation

- family

- a wonderful home

- a wonderful ministry

- good health

- a Bible-teaching church

The third principle, that the last shall be first, I found puzzling. But I was looking at it through man's eyes, rather than taking time to see what God was trying to teach me. We all want to be fair in our dealings with other people and in their dealings with us, yet this passage seemed unfair. Why would the farmer pay the late worker the same amount as the early worker who had been in the fields all day?

In Matthew 20:14 the owner of the farm says, "I want to give the man who was hired last the same as I gave you." To me this represents God's amazing grace and generosity that knows no bounds. What we as man might feel is right is irrelevant. God chooses to do what He chooses to do.

Are we willing to serve God? Our reward is eternal life—even if we come to the field at three o'clock in the afternoon and others have been there since early morning.

> *Father God, search my heart and test my motivation for what I do. Don't let any selfishness enter into my life. You know my intent. May my actions be done with a clear heart. Amen.*

Thoughts for Action

* Write down in your journal why you do what you do.

* Write down at least 10 of your blessings.

* Think of at least two more blessings and write them down too.

* Be willing to freely serve.

Additional Scripture Reading

Matthew 6:33   Mark 10:29-31

☑ ☐ ☐

God Has a Master Plan

Scripture Reading: Jeremiah 18:2-6

Key Verse: Jeremiah 18:6
> O house of Israel, can I not do with you as this potter does?

When our son Brad was in elementary school one of his class projects was to shape clay into something. Brad made a reddish dinosaur-type thing. It's on my bookshelf today as a display of Brad's first work of art—molded and shaped with his small hands, brought home to me with pride.

In high school Brad enrolled in a ceramics class as one of his electives. His first pieces were crooked and misshaped, but as time went on he was able to fashion beautiful works of art. He made vases, pots, pitchers, a butter pot, and many other kinds of pottery. Many pieces of clay were thrown on the wheel to become beautiful but during the process they would take a different direction. Brad would then work and work to reshape them, and sometimes he would have to start all over, working and working again to make each piece just as he wanted it to be.

God has taken, so to speak, a handful of clay in each one of us. He is the Master Potter. We are the vessels in His house. Each one He knows intimately. Each one is different.

We might ask ourselves, "What kind of vessel am I?" Maybe the pot that holds a plant, its roots growing deep in the soil that produces the beauty above in a flowering bloom. Or a cup to hold the tea of friendship. Or a pitcher from which flows the words of wisdom, or a casserole dish with a tightly-sealed lid so nothing from inside will leak out.

Almighty God picks us up like a piece of ugly clay and begins to shape our lives. On the potter's wheel we begin to spin around. God says, "I want you to be strong and beautiful inside and out." The hands of God move up and down as the wheel spins, forming with one hand the inside and with the other the outer side. He says, "I'm with you. I am the Lord of your life, and I will build within you a strong foundation based upon the Word of God."

It feels so good to us as we grow in beauty. Then something happens in our life—a child dies, fire takes our home, we lose our job, our husband leaves, a child rebels. The world cries out to us, "Stop! Jump off the potter's wheel and come with me. I'll give you what you need to feel good." So we place the lid on our vessel and we escape inside ourselves to try to forget the hurt and pain we feel. The beauty God was shaping is put on the shelf only to get dusty and pushed to the back behind all the books and magazines. We feel so lost and far from God as time passes. We've become sidetracked, and yet God has not sidetracked us. He says, "I will never leave you nor forsake you."

I love the bumper sticker I saw, "If you feel far from God, guess who moved?" It wasn't God who placed you on the shelf. *We* are the ones who tighten the lids on our hearts, who put ourselves on the shelf. It's time to push off the lid and jump back on the potter's wheel. We need to become obedient to Almighty God, the Master Potter. He will take the time we were sidetracked and use it to help mold us into His master plan.

In pottery the true beauty of the clay comes out after the firing in the kiln. Allow the Lord to use the negatives in your life to become someone of beauty.

Father God, You truly are the potter and I am the clay. Mold me into the person You want me to be, not what I want to be. I know that is placing a lot of trust in You, but I know that You love me and are concerned about me. May my clay pottery reflect Your light like a fine porcelain vessel. Amen.

Thoughts for Action

❦ Write down in your journal the pain you're feeling today that caused you to place your vessel on the shelf and secure the lid.

❦ Picture yourself pushing off the lid and allowing the Lord to continue healing and reshaping your beautiful vessel.

Additional Scripture Reading

Psalm 73:26   Hebrews 12:7-11
Psalm 121:7

A Marriage Needs Refreshed Inhabitants

Scripture Reading: Proverbs 17:14-22

Key Verse: Proverbs 17:17
> A friend loves at all times, and a brother is born for adversity.

Ed and Carol Neuenschwander (a pastor and his wife) write:

> Although the shell of a union may endure, the spirit of the marriage may disintegrate in time unless mates take periodic and shared reprieves from the pressures they live under.
>
> The pressures we must often escape are not those we create for ourselves, but those brought into our lives from the outside. Nonetheless, they can wear our relationships thin.
>
> The key to keeping a cherished friendship alive may be found in breaking away long enough and frequently enough to keep ourselves fresh and our love growing. And usually that involves childless weekends. Without such moments of focused attention, it's difficult to keep the kind

of updated knowledge of one another that keeps two hearts in close proximity alive and growing together. A growing marriage needs refreshed inhabitants.[6]

We live in a very hectic world that cries out for stillness, quietness, and aloneness. For the sake of our marriage and for our own personal sanities, we must seek solitude.

For the last 21 years my Bob and I have made it a point to get away from all the noises of life and just be by ourselves. We sleep in and disregard clocks. We have no schedules and only limited interruptions. We eat when and if we want. Our favorite time has been from December 27 to January 3. For you this might not be a good time, so choose your own calendar. Get away from everything. Rethink life. Write down some individual and family goals. Be in agreement that these things are a high priority for you and your mate. Under each goal write down what you are going to do to accomplish that desire along with a date when you expect to have it accomplished.

When was the last time you had marital solitude? You've got to make it happen; it just doesn't happen. You must plan to have these special times with your mate. But you say, "We don't have the money!" Don't let excuses sidetrack this desire. Bob and I have found that people do what they want to do. You can find extra money somewhere. If not, start using coupons with your grocery shopping, Put your savings in a special account just for that special time you will have with that special friend—your mate.

Father God, may I learn to be still and know that You are God. I truly want to get off this hectic merry-go-round and be serene and hear the precious words that You give me each day. I want to be refreshed for myself and all those around me. Amen.

Thoughts for Action

❦ Plan a special day and time for your mate. Try to leave your troubles behind and get away for at least one night (two or three if you can).

❦ Set aside a fund for this adventure.

❦ Mail your mate a special letter of invitation.

❦ Keep a modest level of expectation for this time. Too many expectations lead to great disappointments. Try to keep it in perspective. Just let it happen.

Additional Scripture Reading

1 Corinthians 13:3-8   Song of Songs 2:10-13

☑ ☐ ☐

Using Our Talents

Scripture Reading: Matthew 25:14-30

Key Verse: Matthew 25:21
Well done, good and faithful servant!

This passage contains two important points:

- God's call for faithfulness in the use of our talents to Him.

- A warning for those who do not use their talents.

I am continually amazed as I talk to women across America that so many don't realize God can use ordinary people to spread the gospel to those around them.

As a young child growing up behind my mother's dress store, I had no idea that God could use me for much. It wasn't until many years later that God challenged me to take small steps to venture out into this world called "risks" and to be faithful to this calling.

We often think that our talents are going to come out full-grown. However, it is only as we cultivate them that they become mature. As a young seventh-grade girl, I took up playing a beautiful string instrument—the cello. Only after several years of hard practice was I able to play second chair in the Long Beach All City Honors Orchestra.

As with any talent, we must be willing to be used. Yes, there is a risk, but it's worth the insecurity to find out how far God can take us if we are willing. In today's parable we see that the first two servants were willing to take that risk. Their stewardship gave them a blessing of 100-percent return for their efforts, plus their master said, "Well done, good and faithful servant! You have been faithful with a few things; I will put you in charge of many things. Come and share your master's happiness!"

If you want to be successful in God's eyes, you must first be faithful with a few things; then God will cheerfully put you in charge of many things. Is there a talent that people keep telling you you are good at, but you just shrug it off as not being good enough? No one could be blessed by my talent, you think. This passage tells you to take the risk. Don't limit God—He is not to be put into a box. How many of you have a poem to be written, a song to be sung, a book to be authored? Listen to God today as He calls you to a life of adventure. Life is not boring when you have a purpose.

A warning to those who don't use their talents. Even though today's passage talks about faithfulness to use our talents for God, we can't leave this Scripture without looking briefly at God's warning in verses 24-30. This third servant was afraid. He wasn't willing to take a risk with his one talent. He went and buried it in the ground. How many of us are fearful and bury our talents? The warning of these few verses is that God holds us responsible for our lives and what we do with them.

We want to stand before God one day and hear Him say, "Well done, good and faithful servant!"

> *Father God, at times I don't feel I have any talents, but I know You have given each of Your children special gifts. Today I'm asking for direction in using my talents for Your glory. Thank You for listening to my prayer. Amen.*

Thoughts for Action

- Ask God today to reveal to you those special gifts that He wants you to develop.

- Ask a friend to share with you her perception of your own special gifts or talents.

- Develop a plan and a timetable to begin using these talents and gifts for the Lord.

- Be a risk-taker.

Additional Scripture Reading

Exodus 4:10-12   Ephesians 3:14-21

God's Gift

Scripture Reading: John 10:10-18

Key Verse: John 10:10

> *The thief comes only to steal and kill and destroy; I have come that they may have life, and have it to the full.*

———— ❦ ————

One evening we attended a service at an Evangelical Free Church in Fullerton, California. Pastor Chuck Swindoll introduced the speaker for the evening, a man by the name of Ravi Zacharias. His opening statement was "The most dangerous place for a young child today is in his mother's womb." Tears filled my eyes and flooded down my cheeks. I wanted to sob. *Oh, God,* I thought, *what has happened in the world today?* Children are being thrown away as trash, right in our own cities. God says, "Behold children are a gift of the Lord" (Psalm 127:3). We aren't even waiting to unwrap the gift, or allowing the fruit of the womb to be God's reward.

When I held our new little grandson, Bradley Joe II, I saw the miracle of God—a child planted and formed by the Almighty. As I watch our children raise their children, God has impressed upon me the desire to teach women to love and care for children. What a blessing of trust that God would count us women worthy to care for one of His dear children!

Our niece, Becky, and her husband, George, adopted a son. They could never have a child from her womb due to cancer in her body at a very early age. God allowed a child to be born to another woman so Becky and George could be the parents they so desired. This child is sent from God, a gift of God. Thank You, Lord, that this child was not a throwaway, but a child who will contribute much to our society, adopted into a family who wanted a child.

That's exactly what God has for us. He wants to adopt us into His family. We are not God's throwaways. We are His reward. He said, "I have come to give you life" (John 10:10). God sent His Son Jesus as a sacrificed gift to us. He laid down His life for us. Jesus went to the cross so we will never have to suffer the punishment. He took the sins of the world upon Himself and died for you and me.

Thank You, Jesus, for Your love to me that while I was yet a sinner, You died for me. Thank You for the little children. Please protect them in their mother's womb, and may these children be an opened gift to parents. May we, as a country, rise up and defend our children in and out of the womb. Amen.

Thoughts for Action

❦ Ask yourself, "Am I a child of God, adopted into His family?"

❦ If no, ask Jesus into your heart and life now.

❦ Read the whole book of John.

❦ Pray for the child in the mother's womb—for the gift to be opened at its fullness.

Additional Scripture Reading

1 John 1:9	Luke 9:23
Mark 9:37	John 1:12
1 Peter 3:18	

Overload

Scripture Reading: Proverbs 3:1-8

Key Verse: Proverbs 3:6

In all your ways acknowledge him, and he will make your paths straight.

Do you have the type of home where nothing seems to get done? Where each room would take a bulldozer just to clean up the mess? You rush around all day never completing any one job, or if you do complete a task, there is a little one behind you, pulling and messing everything up again! There isn't one of us who *hasn't* experienced these feelings.

When I was 20 our baby daughter Jennifer was six months old. We then took in my brother's three children and within a few months I became pregnant. That gave Bob and me five children under five years old. My life was work, work, work—and yet I never seemed to get anywhere. I was running on a treadmill that never stopped and never moved ahead. I was always tired and never seemed to get enough done, let alone get enough sleep. I was fragmented, totally confused, and stressed.

Then one day during my rushed quiet time with the Lord I read Proverbs 3:6: "In all your ways acknowledge him, and he will make your paths straight." I fell to my knees and prayed, "Please, God, direct my path. I acknowledge You to help me, Lord. I'm going to allow You to lead me and not lead myself in my power. I want Your power and direction. Lord, I'm tired. I'm on overload with husband, home, children, and meals. I have no time left over for me or anyone else. I can't even do any of us justice. Please help me to put it all together and make it work to glorify You and Your children. Amen."

The Lord not only heard my prayer that day, but He honored it as well. I began a program that changed my life. I committed 15 minutes (at least) per day to my quiet time with the Lord. With Brad in hand, I got up earlier each morning. The house was quiet, and my Lord and I talked as I read His Word and prayed.

Next I committed 15 minutes each day to the organization of our home, concentrating on things I never seemed to get done: the silverware drawer, refrigerator, hall closets, photos, bookshelves, piles of papers. I committed to this for 30 days and the pattern was set. God was directing my path. Our home changed dramatically. The cloud of homemaking stress lifted, and I had new direction. The Lord redeemed my time with Him. I had more time to plan meals, make new recipes, play with the children, take walks to the park, even catch a nap from time to time.

Looking back now as a grandparent, I can truly understand the meaning of acknowledging Him in all my ways. It's looking to God for help and comfort in *all* the ways of our life—our families, home, finances, commitments, and careers. God gives us a promise: "I will direct your path."

Father God, sometimes I feel my life is truly on overload. There are days I am confused, frustrated, and misdirected. I come to You on my knees, seeking Your undying patience and the hope You so graciously give. I ask for Your direction in my life. Make order out of disorder. Thank You! Amen.

Thoughts for Action

 Acknowledge Him today.

 Allow Him to direct your path.

 Commit to 15 minutes today to clean something up.

Additional Scripture Reading

Luke 10:40-42   Psalm 139:23-24
Philemon 1:14

❑ ❑ ❑

Spread the Fragrance

Scripture Reading: 2 Corinthians 2:14-17

Key Verse: 2 Corinthians 2:14

> But thanks be to God who always leads us in triumphal procession in Christ and through us spreads everywhere the fragrance of the knowledge of Him.

The dictionary defines "fragrant" as a pleasant odor. The opposite of that would be the smell of a baby's dirty diaper! Yet how sweet the smell of a clean, freshly lotioned and powdered baby after his bath. Baby and mother are happy as the sweet smell permeates the nursery. One baby, two different smells. One you want to hand over to Mom as quickly as you can and the other you want to reach out and pick up from Mom's arms.

Today's Scripture reading says that as we grow in the knowledge of Jesus Christ we become a sweet odor to others. We become a fragrance others want to enjoy and hang around with.

In California, where we live, the orange blossoms in the spring from our orange trees become so potent that the aroma permeates the entire area. The evenings are beautiful with the smell. We keep the bedroom French doors open just to enjoy the fragrance. After a while the blossoms die away and tiny green oranges appear. They slowly grow, and in the late fall those green oranges turn to orange. In December we begin to pick, eat, juice, and give away. But it isn't until late-January, mid-February, that the sugar content is at its height. That's when the fresh orange juice is oh-so-sweet and wonderful. But we never forget the fragrance of the first blooms. Does the fragrance die? Not at all. The smell of that sweet juice is just as wonderful as the blossom.

What is your fragrance? Are you one who others don't want to be around? Or are others wanting to smell the freshness of your sweet spirit because you are a blossom so strong with the fragrance of the spirit of Christ? It takes the knowledge of God's Word to develop that fragrance—learning about God's holy book and the principles taught chapter by chapter.

Where do we begin? We begin with the tiny bloom of time in God's Word, the Bible. A little now, a little later, step-by-step as the months go by we begin to mature just like the orange. We become so full of God's juices that others want to pick us up and squeeze His fragrance from us. The sweetness gets even sweeter as we share His Word with others, pouring out what we've filled our juice pitcher with. As His fragrance enters others' lives, they then begin the same process—a small blossom growing to full maturity. As the process continues from person to person, our orange tree will be full of blossoms, creating a fragrance that can eventually permeate the whole city and eventually the world.

Thoughts for Action

❧ Start today to read God's Holy Bible one chapter per day.

❧ Share with someone the sweet smell you learned.

❧ Pray for God to lead you in triumphal procession to reach the fullness of the sweet fragrance.

Additional Scripture Reading

Galatians 5:22-23   Colossians 1:9-14

Godly Examples

Scripture Reading: Psalm 78:1-7

Key Verse: Psalm 78:4

> *We will not hide them [commandments] from their children; we will tell the next generation the praiseworthy deeds of the Lord, his power, and the wonders he has done.*

A young father was having a talk with his young son as they were preparing to get ready for bed. The father was telling the lad what Christians should be like and how they should act. When Dad had finished describing the attributes of a Christian, the young boy asked a stunning question: "Daddy, have I ever seen a Christian?" The father was aghast. *What kind of an example am I?* he thought.

How would you feel if your child asked you the same question? In our reading today we are given some help to make sure this doesn't happen. This passage establishes some patterns for parenting, patterns we can use to help our children know the things of God and to realize that we are God's children. The writer of Psalm 78 states we can do this by:

- Telling the next generation the praises of the Lord (verse 4).

- Teaching our children the statutes and laws of God (verse 5).

Then our children will see by our words and examples that we are Christians.

In Deuteronomy 6:6-7 Moses said, "These commandments that I give you today are to be upon your hearts. Impress them on your children. Talk about them when you sit at home and when you walk along the road, when you lie down and when you get up."

As parents we are to be reflectors of God to our children. As they look into our faces, our lives, they are to see a man or woman of godly desires and actions. In America today, we earnestly need more parents who will stand up and do the right thing. Christian growth is a daily process of taking off the old self of attitudes, beliefs, and behaviors which reflect the dark side of our nature (sin) and changing to those characteristics that reflect the presence of Christ in our lives. The only way we can grow and succeed in this continuous process is by being renewed in the spirit of our mind (Ephesians 4:22-24). It is a moment-to-moment decision.

By word and by personal example we must train and nurture our children. In this way they can know what a Christian is, because they have known you—the reflector of God's grace.

> *Lord God, I thank You for the godly men and women You have put in my life. They have been a real inspiration to my Christian growth. Help me to continually seek out those godly people who will live the Christian walk in front of me. Amen.*

Thoughts for Action

🍂 Talk to your children today about spiritual things.

🍂 Say a prayer today with your children thanking God for all your blessings.

🍂 Choose today to do one thing that is spiritual (eternal) rather than something that is secular (temporal).

Additional Scripture Reading

Ephesians 6:4   Deuteronomy 6:6-7
Ephesians 4:22-24

□ □ □

Find Favor in God's Eyes

Scripture Reading: Genesis 6:8-22

Key Verse: Genesis 6:8,22

> *Noah found favor in the eyes of the Lord....Noah did everything just as God commanded him.*

Almost every day we can read newspaper articles dealing with people who are being honored by the world:

- government

- sports

- medicine

- education

- theater

- music

On and on we can go. Man finding favor with man. Have you ever thought how much richer it would be to have God find favor with you? I stand in awe when I think of God finding favor in me, but He does. Only through His marvelous grace are we able to come to Him face-to-face.

Noah lived in a world much like today, a world full of sin. Man hasn't changed much over the centuries—we just give sin a different name. Yet through all this wickedness, Noah was a person who lived a godly life. His life was pleasing to God even during those evil days.

Noah didn't find favor because of his individual goodness but through his personal faith in God. We are also judged according to the same standard—that of our personal faith and obedience. My daily prayer is that my family and I will be worthy of the goodness God so richly bestows upon us.

Even though Noah was upright and blameless before God, he wasn't perfect. God recognized that Noah's life reflected a *genuine* faith, not always a *perfect* faith. Do we sometimes feel all alone in our walk with God? Noah walked in greater deprivation than we, yet he still walked with God (verse 9). Noah found that it wasn't the surroundings of his life that kept him in close fellowship with God, but it was the heart of Noah that qualified him to find friendship with God.

How often do we try to find favor with man only to fall on our face in rejection? Noah only wanted to please God. Have you ever asked in that small voice of yours, "Do I find favor in the eyes of the Lord?" When we come to Him and admit we are sinners, we please God. At that time we find God's grace, and we are able to move into a relationship with Jesus Christ. Then we are able to find favor with God.

As we live in this very difficult time of world history, we might ask, "Do I find favor in God's sight?" God gives us grace to live victoriously: "He gives us more grace" (James 4:6).

Father God, oh may I find favor with You.
What an honor for Noah to be favored by You, yet I
realize that he was obedient to Your Word. Give me
a hunger to fall in love with Your Word and put it to
work in my life. You are worthy of praise. Amen.

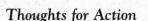

Thoughts for Action

❦ Write down in your journal how you know that you find favor in God's eyes. If you can remember, jot down the exact date you gave your life to Christ.

❦ If you don't think your life finds favor with God, turn to Revelation 3:16. Be assured that by accepting Jesus Christ as your Savior you will find favor with God.

❦ Tell someone today of your new-found favor with God.

❦ Seek out a church if you don't already fellowship with other believers.

❦ Be obedient to God's Word.

Additional Scripture Reading

John 3:16   Philippians 2:12-15
Psalm 19:14

☑ ☐ ☐

Know the Bent of Your Child

Scripture Reading: Proverbs 22:1-16

Key Verse: Proverbs 22:6

*Train a child in the way he should go, and when he is
old he will not turn from it.*

As I think about our children, Brad and Jenny, and look
into the various shades of color in the eyes of our grandchildren, Christine, Chad, Bevan, Bradley Joe II, and Weston, I
see seven unique people. How am I ever going to understand
the uniqueness of each of these children? I know that I have
to attempt to understand each of them if I am going to have
an impact upon molding a healthy, godly character in their
lives. At the heart of each child is a cry, "Please take time to
know me. I am different from anyone else. My sensitivity, my
likes, dislikes, tenderness of heart are different from my
brothers and sisters."

In raising our own children, we saw so many differences
between Jenny and Brad. Even as adults they are still different.
I, in God's wisdom, had to realize that my approach to moti-
vating them had to be styled differently for each of them. Children want to be trained in a personal and tailor-made way.

In our key verse for today, we first see the word "train." In
the Hebrew, this word originally referred to the palate (the

73

roof of the mouth) and to the gums. In Bible times the mid-wife would stick her fingers into a sweet substance and place her fingers into the new child's mouth, creating a sucking desire in the child. The child would then be delicately given to the mother, whereby the child would start nursing. This was the earliest form of "training." The child mentioned in this text can fall between a newborn and a person that is of marrying age.

The second part of this verse is, "when he is old he will not turn from it." At first I thought this meant an older person who had become wayward yet finally returned to the Lord. Little did I know that this word "old" meant "bearded" or "chin." Solomon is talking about a young man who begins to grow a beard when he approaches maturity. For some it might be in junior high school and for others it might be college. The concept is that we as parents are charged to continue training our children as long as they are under our care.

Note that we are to train a child in *his* way—not our way, our plan, our idea. It's important to see that the verse is not a guarantee to parents that raising a child in God's way means he will return back again when he is old. I honestly don't believe this is the proper principle for us as parents. When we train our children according to "his way"—the child's way— we approach each child differently. We don't compare them one to another. Each child is uniquely made.

When I became a student of my two children, I began to design different approaches for each child. Jenny was not Brad, and Brad certainly wasn't Jenny. Each child has his or her own bent and is already established when God places them in our family. God has given you a unique child. Get to know him or her.

> *Father God, You know how much I want to know the bent of my children. Give me the godly wisdom to understand who they are and to be an encouragement to them. Help me to build them up to be all that You designed them to be. Amen.*

Thoughts for Action

❦ Write down in your journal the ways your children are different.

❦ Take into thought how you will train them based on these differences.

❦ Learn one new thing about each of your children today. Do something with that information.

❦ Praise your child today for being uniquely made.

Additional Scripture Reading

Psalm 139:13-16

☑ ☐ ☐

Who's the Older Woman?

Scripture Reading: Titus 2:1-8

Key Verse: Titus 2:4

> Then they can train the younger women to love their
> husbands and children.

When I was younger I wanted to cross Titus 2:4 out of
the Bible. I thought, *I will never be an older woman!* Today I
consider it a privilege to be an older woman. To have the
opportunity to teach another woman is an honor. It doesn't
matter how old we are; we will always be older to someone. I've
overheard Chad at nine years old teaching his young brother
Bevan to play a game, read a book, or count his money.

I've learned much from other women. My mother-in-law,
Gertie Barnes, was a beautiful example to me. I watched her
love her husband, serve him with a soft spirit, nurse him during his last days, and never tire of the task even when her
physical body was exhausted. I'm thankful for her today for
raising such a fine son who has become my wonderful husband.
Actually most of what I am today I learned from the older
women in my life. It's now my joy to teach those very things
to other women God puts before me.

I remember a young woman who came to speak with me
after one of my seminar workshops. She said, "How do I treat
my unsaved husband?" I looked into the beautiful young
brown eyes, "Honey, you treat him as if he were saved." I then

shared with her the great advice I heard at a luncheon when I was a younger bride. I'll never forget this advice and have used it all my married life: "Tell God the negative and tell your husband the positive." Ruth Graham Bell shared a real truth also. "Women," she said, "you will never change your husband. But God can." Yes, Almighty God can change husband, child, and most of all you.

It usually begins with me first. When I begin to change, the other person begins to change. We are the ones who set the thermostats of our homes. When our spirits are warm, loving, peaceful, and soft, others begin to take on the same feeling.

When my Bob would come home from a hot, busy, tiring summer day at the office, I wanted him to find peace and rest as he walked in the door. I worked hard to plan his first 30 minutes at home in the evening. I'd offer him a cold glass of tea or lemonade and allow him a few minutes to change into something comfy and cool. I'd keep the children somewhat settled until Dad could catch his breath and refocus.

Today's working woman can do the same if hubby arrives home before she does. Leave a soft note that says, "Your cold drink is waiting for you in the refrigerator and there are cookies in the jar."

I'm grateful that God has addressed the older woman, because we are the ones who will pass down much wisdom to future generations. I would not be writing books today had it not been for Florence Littauer who mentored me and encouraged me when I was younger to do something I never thought I could possibly do.

> *Father God, let me be an older woman to someone younger today. Oh, how I want to share the truths You have given me about marriage, children, friendship, church, and all the other areas of life. You are worthy of worship and I want to share that with others. Thank You! Amen.*

Thoughts for Action

❦ Be an older woman to someone this week.

❦ Pray for your husband's needs.

❦ Tell your husband today one thing you love about him.

❦ Nurture a teachable spirit in you.

Additional Scripture Reading

Proverbs 31:26   1 Thessalonians 2:7-12

His Name Is Wonderful

Scripture Reading: Isaiah 9:6-7

Key Verse: Isaiah 9:6b
> And he will be called Wonderful Counselor, Mighty God, Everlasting Father, Prince of Peace.

His name is Wonderful, Jesus my Lord. His name is full of wonder, miracles, excitement, fulfillment, peace, and joy. There is something about that name! Our thoughts today must be positive—looking for the good and wonderfulness of the Lord. He is Almighty God who parted the Red Sea, raised Lazarus from the dead, and lives today in our hearts, wanting to be a miracle in our life.

As Isaiah wrote, "Of the increase of his government or peace there will be no end."

The peace of Jesus is in our hearts. God didn't promise joy, but He did say He would increase our peace.

To be sure, life will bring sorrow, broken hearts, health problems, financial difficulties, and much, much more. Our life in and with our Lord will bring dependence, maturity, refreshment, refuge, redemption, righteous judgment, and many rewards. Plus, He will restore your heart, mind, and soul.

Take your problems and worries of today, wrap them in a box, and close the lid very tightly. Then, my dear, put it into the wonderful hands of Jesus. Now walk away and don't take it back. Eighty percent of the things we worry about never happen anyway—so let Jesus take the remaining 20 percent. He will give back to you 100 percent of His life and peace. In fact, He has done it already for you as He hung on the cross of Calvary.

Let's sing His wonderful name: Jesus, Jesus, Jesus. There is just something about that name!

> *Father God, You have so many wonderful names. May I search out the Scripture and really get to know You by Your names. Each one has a special meaning and gives me deeper understanding to who You are. Reveal Your character to me today. Amen.*

Thoughts for Action

❦ In your journal, make a list of your worries today.

❦ Imagine putting them in a box—all of them.

❦ Now burn or throw the box away.

❦ Expect a miracle from our Wonderful God.

❦ List your blessings, naming them one by one.

❦ Use a page in your journal to write down all the various names of God as your read them in Scripture.

Additional Scripture Reading

Philippians 4:8   Psalm 23:6
Psalm 136:1

I'm Special Because

Scripture Reading: Psalm 139:13-17

Key Verse: Psalm 139:14
> *I praise you because I am fearfully and wonderfully made; your works are wonderful, I know that full well.*

One evening our seven-year-old grandson, Chad, was helping me set the dinner table. Whenever the grandchildren come over, we have a tradition of honoring someone at the table with our red plate that says, "You Are Special Today" (even though it isn't a birthday, anniversary, or other special occasion). It was natural for me to ask Chad, "Who should we honor today with our special plate?" Chad said, "How about *me?* "Yes, Chad, you are special," I replied. "It's your day."

He was so proud as we all sat around the table and said our blessing. Then Chad said, "I think it would be very nice if everyone around the table would tell me why they think I'm special." Bob and I got a chuckle out of that, but we thought it might be a good idea, so we did it. After we were all through Chad said, "Now I want to tell you why I think I'm special. I'm special because I'm a child of God." Chad was so right on. Psalm 139:13-14 tells us that God knew us before we were born. He knit us together in our mother's womb and we are wonderfully made.

When I was seven, 10, or even 22, I could not have told anyone why I was special. I didn't even talk, I was so shy. My alcoholic father would go into a rage, swearing and throwing things. I was afraid I'd say the wrong thing, so I didn't talk. My self-image wasn't too good. But the day came when I read Psalm 139, and my heart came alive with the realization that I, too, am special because I am a child of God. And so are you. We were uniquely made as He knit us together in our mother's womb.

Verse 16 says, "All the days are ordained for me." It's not by accident you are reading this devotion today. Perhaps you, too, need to know how very special you are. We have all been given unique qualities, talents, and gifts. And you, my dear one, have been made by God. You are His child. He loves you more than any earthly father could possibly love you. Because He is your Heavenly Father, Almighty God, He cares for you even when you don't care for yourself. You are His child even when you feel far from Him. It's never your Heavenly Father who moves away from you. It's you who moves away from Him.

Today is ordained by God for you to draw near to Him and allow Him to be near to you. Because today is your day, my friend, "You Are Special Today." A child of God, as Chad said.

> *Father God, thank You for making me so special, with a heart to love You more and more each day. Please today help me to draw near to You and to feel Your presence. Thank You for being my Heavenly Father. I know that I'm never alone. You are always with me. Amen.*

Thoughts for Action

❦ Tell someone why you are special today.

❦ Ask someone why he or she is special.

❦ Write a note in your journal to God and thank Him for who you are, His special child.

Additional Scripture Reading

Psalm 73:28	Ephesians 1:11
Ephesians 1:4	Proverbs 31:29

Children Are a Reward from God

Scripture Reading: Psalm 127:1-5

Key Verse: Psalm 127:3

Sons are a heritage from the Lord, children a reward from him.

Our children are continually reaching out to see if Mom and Dad really love them. When are we going to learn to say, "I love you and I am very proud of you"? They long to hear those words, and they will continue to test us until they hear *and* believe those words from us.

- They yell and scream in the grocery store.
- They have temper tantrums in the restaurant.
- They wear strange clothes.
- They have funny haircuts in odd colors.
- They use vulgar language.
- They run away from home.
- They get bad grades in school.
- They run around with friends that you don't approve of.

In these unacceptable behaviors, they are indirectly asking, "Do you approve of me?" And they aren't hearing your response.

We had a good friend whose son was not into sports and athletics like his dad desired. He was into motocross racing. The parents came to our pastor, and the dad asked the pastor what he should do. The pastor, not surprisingly, said, "Take up motocrossing!" The dad predictably said, "I don't like...

- dirt

- grease

- motorcycles

- the crowd

- etc.!

The pastor replied, "How much do you love your son? Enough to get grease on your hands and clothes?" The next week Dad was off with his son to the local motocross event. Soon after they were involved with dirt, grease, and different people. Through these actions Dad showed his son that he really loved him more than anything else, even if everything wasn't the way Dad would have liked.

We need to understand that our sons and daughters are a heritage from the Lord and that children are a reward from God. And we need to start living as though we believe it.

> *Father God, may You reveal to me today that my children are a reward from You. Sometimes I get so discouraged that I want to throw in the towel. I'm looking forward to some special encouragement from You today. Amen.*

Thoughts for Action

 Write your children a note letting them know how much you love them. Give a few specific traits you like about them. (Do it even if your children are young.)

 Make a point to spend quality one-on-one time with each of your children.

 Place a note on your calendar next month to do it again.

Additional Scripture Reading

    Psalm 128:1-3   Genesis 33:5
    Psalm 127:4-5

The Quiet Spirit

Scripture Reading: 1 Peter 3:1-9

Key Verse: 1 Peter 3:4

> *Instead, it should be that of your inner self, the unfading beauty of a gentle and quiet spirit, which is of great worth in God's sight.*

It's been a tough day. You were late getting off work, the children need picking up at day care, you have no clue as to what to have for dinner, and the car needs gas. Stopping at the market to pick up some kind of food is a disaster—the checkout lines are long and the checkers are slow. Finally you get home, kick off the shoes from your aching feet, and throw the food on the stove, turning it up high to cook faster for starving and cranky children. The phone rings and the dog barks while the children cry for dinner. Are you supposed to have a quiet and gentle spirit? You probably don't even want one.

You know what I used to do on days like that? I would go into the bathroom, stick my head in the toilet, and cry to God, "If You only knew what it's like out there, You wouldn't let me be in this situation." Sometimes I would have to make two or three trips in and out of the bathroom until I could settle down enough to say, "Lord, help me!" I would then count to 10, take a deep breath, and attack.

You know how you can avoid days like this? By making a plan for just those kind of days! Plan ahead by preparing make-ahead freezer meals, getting gas in the car before it reaches empty, and having on hand a quick, pre-dinner snack for the children—pretzels, popcorn, a few crackers and cheese, or a frozen smoothie.

It's not God who gives the confusion. It's our own mismanagement of time and organization.

The quiet spirit comes as we plan to eliminate the stress in our life. We must learn to slow down and refocus our goals and priorities.

There was a woman in my Bible study who had 10 children. Jeanette was worn out physically. She needed dental work and a good haircut. Her clothes didn't fit, and her shoes were worn over on the heels. Yet she came to the study every week by bus, and she was always prepared. She added great spiritual depth to the class. This busy, overworked mother had a beautiful inner spirit, and after our first study together, none of us saw the outside of Jeanette. We saw and felt her inner spirit, the gentle and quiet spirit that never complained or blamed God for a drug-dependent husband who wasn't working. She was absolutely beautiful. God honored her heart. Today Jeanette has victory in her life and so does her husband.

Thoughts for Action

❧ Praise God for a gentle and quiet spirit of a godly woman.

❧ Plan your meals for the week.

❧ Check the gas gauge.

❧ Think of several ways you can work toward a gentle and quiet spirit.

Additional Scripture Reading

Psalm 37:3-8   1 John 5:14-15

Offer Hospitality

Scripture Reading: 1 Peter 4:1-11

Key Verse: 1 Peter 4:9

Offer hospitality to one another without grumbling.

My mother, at 77, lived in a one-room efficiency apartment on the fifteenth floor of a senior citizen building. She continually shared hospitality with a cup of tea, a cookie, a piece of carrot cake or banana bread. Her guests always felt special sipping tea in a real china tea cup, eating cookies placed on a pretty plate with a paper doily, and enjoying a few flowers on the table with a lit candle.

Do you grumble at the thought of inviting guests into your home? Many of today's women seem to avoid hospitality due to the pressure of their busy lives.

It didn't take much for Mama to be hospitable. One cup of tea, one cookie. Hospitality is the act of caring for one another. We can entertain all we like, but not until we care does it become hospitality.

So many times we feel things have to be perfect—the right time, a clean house, the right food. Yet today's Scripture tells us to cheerfully share our homes. When was the last time you had guests over?

Our daughter Jenny has a hard-working husband, who is a painting contractor, and a busy home to care for. Often Bill will ask Jenny if a meeting or a party can be held at their home. Jenny has every reason to grumble, yet she joyfully whips a buffet together, sometimes asking the guests to bring a dish—which they are happy to contribute. (By the way, Jenny gets a lot of great recipes from the potluck entertaining.)

Some people have a gift of serving others through hospitality, but I've found one thing to be true: Hospitality can be taught. Also, the more you entertain, the easier it becomes. Some of the best times in our home have been the simplest.

One very busy working mom discovered the way to fast, convenient hospitality. On her way home from work she picked up a bunch of flowers and frozen lasagna from the freezer department of the supermarket, which she threw in her own casserole dish. She tossed a prepared salad in her wooden bowl, bought a frozen cake for dessert, and lit a candle. Within moments she served a lovely dinner to guests who later helped clean up the kitchen, exclaiming, "This has been a delightfully delicious evening."

No one knew she didn't work hours preparing the meal. We can do whatever we want to do however we want to do it.

First Peter 4:11 says that if anyone serves he should do it with the strength God provides. God will provide the strength as we provide the desire. Jesus often fed people before He preached. Having friends in our home gives us the opportunity to let them see Jesus in us, to feel our spirits, to be touched by our love and caring. Many doors have been opened in the hearts of our friends when we've shared a meal together.

> *Father God, put a hunger in my heart to have people in my home. I want to learn to break bread with those around me, as Jesus did. You know I often don't feel confident in offering hospitality to others, but I ask You for courage to take a risk in this area of my life. Amen.*

Thoughts for Action

❧ List those you can invite to your home.

❧ Call and invite someone on your list today.

❧ Don't panic—plan instead. Make it simple.

❧ Pray that God will use it as you serve Him through hospitality.

Additional Scripture Reading

Philippians 4:13   1 Timothy 5:9-10
Romans 12:13

*Just as the
lovely flowers lend
their sweetness to
each day, may we
touch the lives
of those we meet
in a kind
and gentle way.*

The Lord Is
My Shepherd

Scripture Reading: Psalm 23:1-6

Key Verse: Psalm 23:4

Even though I walk through the valley of the shadow of death, I will fear no evil, for you are with me; your rod and your staff, they comfort me.

It was a cool February evening in California. My 88-year-old Jewish Auntie's hospital room had its lights dimmed to gray. It had been a few days since I had seen her. We had had such a nice visit then. She was alert as we talked about family and how she missed Uncle Hy, who had passed away nine months earlier. Now she lay there so thin and frail. Her breathing was heavy and irregular.

As I sat by her bedside, holding her cool, clammy hand, I thought of the other times I had seen her in similar situations. Auntie had had surgery 25 years earlier, and because of complications, she almost died. A few years later she was a passenger in a car that rolled down a steep hill and hit a power pole. Her face had been smashed, her jaw and nose broken, and other complications set in. Again, she almost died. As life went on, illnesses came and went, but mostly came. The doctors had already told us three times in the past year that

Auntie wouldn't make it through the night. But she always did. Was this February night going to be any different? The doctor had been in to check on her and just shook his head. The rabbi arrived to look in for a visit with no response from Auntie. Would this be the night she would give up her fight for life?

On the other side of the curtain that was three-quarters drawn between us and the bed on the other half of the room there was a charming, late-middle-aged Jamaican woman who was almost blind and suffered from diabetes. She spoke eight languages and had a sweet sense of peace and joy about her in spite of her pain. We enjoyed talking with her and found out that she was a Christian believer who grew up learning to read from the Bible. Every night before she closed her eyes to sleep she would recite Psalm 23. On sleepless nights she would repeat it over and over again. As she talked, I felt our spirits meet, and she would tell me how Auntie's day had gone. In only a few hours with her I knew I loved that woman.

Bob and I were both tired as the clock read 11 P.M. that February night. We'd had a busy day in the office and had driven almost two hours through Los Angeles traffic to be with Auntie.

By now Auntie's breathing was very labored. I leaned over to pat her forehead and give her a last hug goodbye. My lips were by her ear when the Spirit of God began to speak from my lips, "The Lord is my Shepherd, I shall not want." Then the angel from "bed B" joined me: "He makes me lie down in green pastures." It was like the sound of a million voices surrounding the room. "Even though I walk through the valley of the shadow of death, I will fear no evil, for you are with me; your rod and your staff, they comfort me." That precious black woman and I dueted to the end of the psalm. "You prepare a table before me in the presence of my enemies. You anoint my head with oil; my cup overflows. Surely goodness and love will follow me all the days of my life, and I will dwell in the house of the Lord forever."

With a last kiss Bob and I walked out of the hospital room forever. Thirty minutes later Auntie died, with the words of the Twenty-third Psalm surrounding her room.

> *Father God, I do want to trust in You during all the various times of my life. Help me to realize in good health that You are my shepherd so that in bad times I can trust You to take care of me. You are such a wonderful guardian of all of my life. Amen.*

Thoughts for Action

- Memorize Psalm 23.

- Share it with a friend this week.

- Thank God for David, who wrote these beautiful words and truly knew the meaning of each verse.

- Call a friend who might need encouragement and tell her that you are thinking and praying for her today.

Additional Scripture Reading

Psalm 40:11   Revelation 7:17
Psalm 36:8

How Careless

Scripture Reading: Proverbs 16:16-28

Key Verse: Proverbs 16:18
> Pride goes before destruction, a haughty spirit before a fall.

Candi's dad gave her husband, Vinnie, a Rolex watch. But Vinnie had trouble wearing it because of the weight, size, and discomfort on his wrist. So during the day he would take it off and set it on his desk at work, planning to exchange the watch for something more to his liking as soon as he could. Would you believe that one day when he went to lunch the watch was stolen off his desk? Unfortunately, Vinnie was not able to claim insurance on it even close to its true value.

How mindless, Candi thought. *I can't believe he was so careless as to leave such an expensive watch laying around on his desk.* She was angry with him about the loss, thinking to herself, *I would never do anything like that.*

A few weeks later Candi was picking up her children at school. In a hurry and distracted by the errands, schedules, and church projects to be done, she mindlessly jumped out of her car, leaving the window down and her purse sitting on the front seat. After collecting her girls and jumping back into the car, away she went. She stopped at a drive-through window to buy a treat for the girls, and—you guessed it—her purse was gone, stolen out of her car in front of the school.

Angry and feeling frustrated with herself, she couldn't wait to get home and make the calls to credit card companies. She soon discovered the thief had already charged $500 worth of goods on her cards.

Candi began to realize how she had treated her husband so badly when she herself had done the same careless act. When Vinnie returned home, she didn't wait to apologize to him for her attitude—and she confessed her careless act as well.

What a great lesson for all of us—treating others as we want to be treated. That old motto has certainly proven to be true over our years, "What goes around comes around."

Thoughts for Action

❦ Does someone need an apology from you? If so, who? Do it today. Write a letter, make a phone call, whatever it takes.

❦ Take your time. It will avoid careless mistakes.

❦ Hug your husband today—just for a hug's sake.

❦ When someone makes a mistake, think of how you would like to be treated should you be in their shoes. Keep this in mind.

❦ Write love notes using a heart (❤) where the "o" in "love" goes.

Additional Scripture Reading

1 John 1:9   Psalm 51:10
1 Peter 5:6-7

A Heritage from the Lord

Scripture Reading: Psalm 127:1–128:4

Key Verse: Psalm 127:3
Sons are a heritage from the Lord, children a reward from him.

In a recent Bible study that I was in, the teacher asked us, "Did you feel loved by your parents when you were a child?" Many remarked:

- "They were too busy for me."
- "I spent too much time with the babysitters."
- "Dad took us on trips, but he played golf all the time we were away."
- "I got in their way. I wasn't important to them."
- "Mom was too involved at the country club to spend time with us."
- "Mom didn't have to work, but she did just so she wouldn't have to be home with us children."
- "A lot of pizzas came to our house on Friday nights when my parents went out for the evening."

I was amazed at how many grown women expressed ways they *didn't* feel loved in their homes growing up. What would your children's answers be if someone asked them the same question?

Today's Scripture reading gives an overview of what it takes to make and develop a close-knit and healthy family. We first look at the foundation of the home in verse 1: "Unless the Lord builds the house, its builders labor in vain. Unless the Lord watches over the city, the watchmen stand guard in vain."

The protective wall surrounding a city was the very first thing to be constructed when a new city was built. The men of the Old Testament knew they needed protection from the enemy, but they were also smart enough to know that walls could be climbed over, knocked down, or broken apart. Ultimately, the people knew that their real security was the Lord guarding the city.

Today we must return to that trust in the Lord, if we are going to be able to withstand the destruction of our "walls"—the family. As I drive the Southern California freeways, I see parents who are burning the candle at both ends to provide for all the material things they think will make their families happy. We rise early and retire late. In Psalm 127:2 we find this is futile. Our trust must be that the Lord has His hand over our families. The business of our hands are only futile efforts to satisfy those we love.

In verse 3 we see that, "Children are a reward [gift] from the Lord." In the Hebrew, "gift" means "property," "a possession." Truly, God has loaned us His property or possessions to care for and to enjoy for a certain period of time.

My Bob loves to grow vegetables in his "raised-bed" garden each summer. I am amazed at what it takes to get a good crop. He cultivates the soil, sows seeds, waters, fertilizes, weeds, and prunes. Raising children takes a lot of time, care, nurturing, and cultivating as well. We can't neglect these responsibilities if we are going to produce good fruit. Left to itself, the garden—and our children—will grow into weeds.

Bob always has a big smile on his face when he brings a big basket full of corn, tomatoes, cucumbers, and beans into the kitchen. As the harvest is Bob's reward, so children are parents' reward.

As we move on to Psalm 127:4-5, we see a picture of how to handle our children. They are compared to arrows in the hands of a warrior. Skill in handling an arrow is vital. Wise parents will know their children, understand them, examine them before they shoot them into the world. When I was in high school, I took an archery class and I soon learned that I wasn't Robin Hood. I found archery much more difficult than basketball, and it was more dangerous if not done properly. Shooting a straight arrow and hitting a target was a lot harder in real life than what I saw at the movies or on TV. Proper parenting takes a lot of skill. It's not a one-shot experience.

In our last section of this passage, Psalm 128:1-3, we dwell upon the importance of the Lord's presence in the home.

- The Lord is central to a home's happiness (verse 2).

- Through the Lord, wives will be a source of beauty and life to the home (verse 3a).

- Through the Lord, children will flourish like olive trees, which generously provide food, oil, and shelter for others (verse 3b).

Let your home reflect a place where its members come to be rejuvenated after a very busy time away from it. Say "no" when you are tempted to just become a harried taxi driver, delivering the family from one activity to the next. God has a better plan. He wants you to walk in His ways.

Father God, slow me down so I can spend
valuable time with my family. Help me to realize
that our children will only be with us for such a

short time, and that what I do to and with them
will affect their children's lives too. What an awesome responsibility! I can't wait to be with them
today. Amen.

Thoughts for Action

❧ Reflect upon this statement: "Our attitude toward our
children reveals our attitude toward God."

❧ Stop and take time to listen to your children, eye-to-eye.

❧ Be consistent in your training on what's right and what's
wrong.

❧ Give your child a beautiful gift today—TIME!

Additional Scripture Reading

James 1:19-20	Proverbs 18:10
Matthew 18:5-6	Proverbs 16:24

A Wisdom Only God Can Provide

Scripture Reading: Proverbs 3:11-12; 13:24; 15:13; 17:22; 22:15; 29:15

Key Verse: Proverbs 15:13
> A happy heart makes the face cheerful, but heartache crushes the spirit.

With all the media attention given to child abuse, we as Christian parents become confused regarding the area of discipline. The book of Proverbs, fortunately, contains some specific verses which offer good biblical principles for raising our children.

We often feel we are in a tug-of-war between child and parent. The natural tendency is to throw in the towel and give up. Far too often we have seen parents who have given up this task to gently yet firmly shape their child's will, as would a trainer of a wild animal or as the potter would a piece of clay. Dr. James Dobson, in his book *The Strong-Willed Child*, gives some insight into this area:

> It is obvious that children are aware of the contest of wills between generations, and that is precisely why the parental response is so important. When a child behaves in ways that are

disrespectful or harmful to himself or others, his hidden purpose is often to verify the stability of the boundaries. This testing has much the same function as a policeman who turns doorknobs at places of business after dark. Though he tries to open doors, he hopes they are locked and secure. Likewise, a child who assaults the loving authority of his parents is greatly reassured when their leadership holds firm and confident. He finds his greatest security in a structured environment where the rights of other people (and his own) are protected by definite boundaries.[7]

It takes a special kind of person with godly wisdom to provide this kind of balance. How do we accomplish this? First, we must note there is a difference between *abuse* and *discipline*. Proverbs 13:24 tells us that if we truly love our children, we'll discipline them diligently. Abuse is unfair, extreme, and degrading. This action doesn't grow out of love, but from hate. Abuse leads to a soiled self-image that will often last a lifetime. Discipline, on the other hand, upholds the child's worth and is fair and fitting for the infraction.

Second, we must be sure the child understands the discipline he is to receive. When we disciplined Jenny and Brad, we spent a lot of time with them discussing what they did and making sure they understood what the infraction was. We realize that every child is different, so the way you approach them will be through your knowledge of that child. In our day, we didn't have "Time Out." However, we've found this to be a very good technique, and we use it with our grandchildren very effectively. There are times, though, when a sterner approach is necessary, and on occasions we did give spankings. They were firmly applied to the beefy part of the buttocks, and they did hurt.

In reality, this was very rarely done and never in anger—always in stern, tough love. After each such encounter we met with the child, reviewed why he was disciplined, and talked about how his actions might be altered in the future. One of our main purposes was to have the child remember that he is responsible for his actions and must be accountable for his behavior. After every time we disciplined our children, we ended in prayer and warm hugs and assuring words. This form of correction strengthens the child's self-image. It builds his spirits up when he knows his boundaries. Our love and concern for both our kids and their well-being created stronger motivation for them to behave according to our family's conduct and behavior standards.

Third, we want to shape and not crush our children's spirit. You can look into the eyes of children around you to see those who are being crushed and those being shaped.

> A happy heart makes the face [eyes] cheerful, but heartache crushes the spirit (Proverbs 15:13).

Our goal as a parent is to build up our children with solid direction and self-assurance that will see them throughout life. The child that is shaped will have a love for life, but a crushed spirit produces a child with no hope for the future.

Fourth, we must always keep balance in our lives. We don't want to be so rigid that we don't allow members in our family to make mistakes, or so loose that family members are bouncing off the walls trying to find their boundaries. Children must know where the boundaries are and what the consequences are if they choose to go beyond these limits.

In Scripture we read about physical discipline, such as using the rod. Naturally, none of us wants to risk being an abusive parent.

> Folly is bound up in the heart of a child; but the rod of discipline will drive it far from him (Proverbs 22:15).

Dr. Dobson underscores the importance of a child being able to associate wrongdoing with pain:

> If your child has ever bumped his arm against a hot stove, you can bet he'll never deliberately do that again. He does not become a more violent person because the stove burnt him; in fact, he learned a valuable lesson from the pain. Similarly, when he falls out of his high chair or smashes his finger in the door or is bitten by a grumpy dog, he learns about physical dangers in his world. These bumps and bruises throughout childhood are nature's way of teaching him what to fear. They do not damage his self-esteem. They do not make him vicious. They merely acquaint him with reality. In like manner, an appropriate spanking from a loving parent provides the same service. It tells him there are not only physical dangers to be avoided but he must steer clear of some social traps as well (selfishness, defiance, dishonesty, unprovoked aggression, etc.).[8]

Fifth, be consistent in your approach to guiding and directing your children. Several of these have already been discussed:

- Make sure there is a clear understanding of the rules.
- Discipline in private. If you're in a public setting, wait until you can be alone.
- Review the infraction and its consequences.
- Be firm in your discipline.
- Assure your child of your love and concern.

- Hold your child firmly after each discipline.

- End your session with a time of prayer. (Give your child an opportunity to pray too.)

As Bob and I look back over those training years, we made plenty of mistakes. But when we did, we were the first to admit them to our children. Even when you miss the mark occasionally, you still are moving in a proper direction. If you don't have a goal or direction in this area of your life, you will miss the mark totally. Be encouraged. Your children want to know their boundaries. There is self-assurance in knowing.

Thoughts for Action

❦ Do you have a clear direction in your life regarding your children's discipline? If not, spend some time today thinking about it and possibly write down some of your ideas in your journal.

❦ If you are married, you may want to review these ideas with your mate.

❦ Tell each member in your family today that you love them, and state why you do.

Additional Scripture Reading

Mark 12:28-31	1 Peter 5:5-6
Galatians 5:16	Colossians 3:17

Choose to Be Thankful

Scripture Reading: Ephesians 5:15-20

Key Verse: Ephesians 5:20

> ...always giving thanks to God the Father for everything, in the name of our Lord Jesus Christ.

I love to travel. In our ministry, I get the great opportunity to travel to various regions in America and Canada. While in the South and Midwest, I love to have the children come up and address me, "Mrs. Emilie" and to offer a polite gesture of "thank you." It not only tells me a lot regarding the child and that region of our country, but also the teaching that the parent has given to that child.

I would do almost anything for a person who has proper manners and a thankful heart. And if I'm that way as a human being, how much more God must be overjoyed when one of His children responds with a thankful heart. There are two kinds of people in the world: the givers and the takers. It seems like today there are more takers than ever before. We drastically need people with thankful hearts.

In Galatians 5:22 we read a list of Christian characteristics that are universally known as the "fruit of the Spirit." They are: love, joy, peace, patience, kindness, goodness, faithfulness, gentleness, and self-control. Being thankful is not on this list. Evidently to be thankful comes about by choice. We *choose* to be thankful. Have you made that choice today?

We're encouraged to be "always giving thanks to God ...for everything" (Ephesians 5:20). That means everything from the littlest to the biggest. I have made thanksgiving a part of my lifestyle. In the morning upon waking, I thank God for another day, for my health, and for purpose for life. In the evening upon retiring, I thank God for watching over me, giving me a meaningful day, and providing safety, food, and shelter. The psalmist expresses it like this, "To proclaim your love in the morning and your faithfulness at night" (Psalm 92:2).

An example of a lady who understands the true meaning of having a thankful heart is reflected in this short excerpt:

> The room is clean, even airy; a bright little fire burns in the grate; and in a four-post bed you will see sitting up a woman of sixty-four years of age, with her hands folded and contracted, and her whole body crippled and curled together as the disease cramped it, and rheumatism has fixed it for eight and twenty years. For sixteen of these years, she has not moved from her bed, or looked out of the window, or even lifted her hand to her own face; and also is in constant pain, while she cannot move a limb. But listen! She is so thankful that God has left her that great blessing, the use of one thumb! Her left hand is clinched and stiff, and utterly useless; but she has a two-pronged fork fastened to a stick, with which she can take off her great old-fashioned spectacles, and put them on again, with amazing effort. By the same means, she can feed herself; and she can sip her tea through a tube, helping herself with this one thumb. And there is an other thing she can accomplish with her fork; she can turn over the leaves of a large Bible when placed within her reach. A recent

visitor addressed her with the remark, that she was all alone. "Yes," she replied in a peculiarly sweet and cheerful voice, "I am alone, and yet not alone."—"How is that?"—"I feel that the Lord is constantly with me."—"How long have you lain here?"—"For sixteen years and four months; and for two years and four months I have not been lifted out of my bed to have it made: yet I have much to praise and bless the Lord for."—"What is the source of your happiness?"—"The thought that my sins are forgiven, and dwelling on the great love of Jesus my Savior. I am content to lie here so long as it shall please him that I should stay, and to go whenever he shall call me."

Here is a truly divine example of a woman with a thankful heart.

Start today if you aren't already—be thankful.

> *Father God, bring to my mind all that I need to be thankful for. I sometimes get so hurried and hassled that I don't still my heart and know that You are God. At this moment I say thank You, thank You. Amen.*

Thoughts for Action

❧ Jot down in your journal 10 things for which you are thankful.

❧ Call someone today who means a lot to you and tell her how thankful you are for her friendship.

❧ Write a note of thanks to someone today: a friend, a family member, a pastor, an instructor.

❦ Tell God tonight before you go to bed how thankful you are for Him.

Additional Scripture Reading

Hebrews 13:15   1 Thessalonians 5:16-18
Colossians 3:17

Our life is
like a garden,
and with God's
loving care
it blossoms
with the flowers
of His blessings
everywhere.

Stop and Come

Scripture Reading: Genesis 22:1-18

Key Verse: Genesis 22:8

Abraham answered, "God himself will provide the lamb for the burnt offering, my son." And the two of them went on together.

———— ❧ ————

There were two words we were firm about teaching our children when they were growing up: "Stop" and "Come." If you think about it, you probably use these words often with your own children. Children who learn them will be obedient people. I can honestly say the one thing our children learned was obedience. It has and is paying off, even in their adult lives.

Abraham is a beautiful example of obedience to his Father God. God tested Abraham to the limit of obedience. God called his name, "Abraham." Abraham *stopped* and replied, "Here I am, Lord." Then God instructed Abraham to take his only son to Moriah. There Abraham was to sacrifice Isaac as a burnt offering on one of the mountains. I wonder what Abraham thought. He loved Isaac so much. Isaac was the son of Sarah, who had prayed for many years for a child. Sarah had been in her nineties when she gave birth. Isaac was a miracle child, so wanted and so loved. Abraham knew God intimately. He had experienced the mighty power of God when He gave them Isaac in their later years. Now God was telling Abraham to sacrifice Isaac.

———— ❦ ————

Early in the morning after God spoke to Abraham, Abraham took Isaac, saddled up his donkey, and along with two servants headed up to the mountain in Moriah. After cutting enough wood for the burnt offering, they set out as God had told him. "On the third day Abraham looked up and saw the place in the distance. He said to his servants, 'Stay here with the donkey while I and the boy go over there. We will worship and then *we* will come back to you'" (Genesis 22:5, emphasis added).

"*We* will worship. *We* will come back." Abraham believed God. He trusted God, and he kept moving ahead in obedience to God. I'm sure the servants and Isaac were puzzled. Where was the sacrifice? The servants didn't ask. Isaac didn't ask.

"Abraham took the wood for the burnt offering and placed it on his son Isaac, and he himself carried the fire and the knife" (verse 6). Isaac obviously wasn't a small child—he was big enough to carry heavy wood up a mountain. So I would guess he was probably pre- or early teens.

As father and son walked up the mountain, they probably talked together. "Isaac spoke up and said to his father Abraham, 'Father?' 'Yes my son,' Abraham replied. 'The fire and the wood are here,' Isaac said, 'but where is the lamb for the burnt offering?'" (verse 7). I'm sure Isaac was a bit puzzled. *We have everything but the lamb,* he may have thought. *Where will we ever find a lamb up here in the wilderness?*

I love Abraham's reply: "God himself will provide the lamb for the burnt offering, my son" (verse 8). And the two of them went on together. When they reached the place God had told Abraham about, he went to work, removing the wood from Isaac's back. He built an altar for worship and then arranged the wood on top. This was the ultimate of worshiping God—an altar built by hand and an offering of obedience.

Then Abraham said, "Come," to Isaac, and he placed him on top of the wood and bound him on the altar. Isaac was also obedient. He must have learned this from Abraham. Isaac came to his own father who he loved and trusted—his father who loved and trusted Father God. While the Bible doesn't say anything about Isaac's words or thoughts, I'm sure he was very frightened. But perhaps he knew, too, that God would provide. Maybe Isaac was willing to die for God. I don't know, but there was Isaac—bound on top of the wood he had carried himself.

Abraham had the knife. Everything was prepared and ready. "Then [Abraham] reached out his hand and took the knife to slay his son" (verse 10). When an animal is sacrificed as an offering to God, it is bound on the altar of wood and the knife is plunged into the throat and sliced down the middle through the stomach. Abraham's arm was lifted up, ready to plunge the knife into his only son's throat when "the angel of the LORD called out to him from heaven 'Abraham! Abraham!'" (verse 11). Abraham *stopped*. "'Do not lay a hand on the boy,' he said. 'Do not do anything to him. Now I know that you fear God, because you have not withheld from me your son, your only son. Abraham looked up and there in a thicket he saw a ram caught by its horns. He went and took the ram and sacrificed it as a burnt offering instead of his son" (verses 12-13). I'm sure Isaac must have thought, *That was a close call, Dad.*

Abraham named that place on top of the mountain "The Lord Will Provide." There was no doubt in Abraham's heart that God would provide. Can you imagine what the two servants must have thought when they saw Abraham and Isaac come back with no wood and a blood-stained knife? But then Abraham did say, "*We* will return." They did worship, and they did return. I know my worship today is stronger because of this passage. I'm sure Abraham and Isaac's was as well.

Isaac showed obedience when his father said, "*Come* with me to worship," and "*Come* get on the pile of wood." Abraham showed obedience, and he experienced in a truly deep and unique way that the Lord will provide. When the angel called his name, Abraham stopped to listen.

Perhaps our cup needs to be filled with an obedience like Abraham's. We say we trust God, but then we take matters into our own hands and try to move ahead in our own power, not allowing the Lord to provide. We miss seeing and experiencing the miracle hand of God.

What are you asking God to provide for you today? Job, children, husband, finances? Are you willing to trust Him and know He will provide? How obedient are we to God's call? Come! Come to His altar and lay the pain of your heart there. Stop and worship. And as you walk away from your worship with God, you will know with hope and trust that God says, "I will provide."

Thoughts for Action

❦ Make a worship center in your home—a chair where you pray, a corner of a room, a closet, a bathroom, under a tree, by the creek, at the kitchen table.

❦ Come and worship.

❦ Stop and listen.

❦ Trust God.

❦ Obey His Word.

Additional Scripture Reading

Galatians 4:28   Romans 9:7
Hebrews 11:17-19

How to Preserve a Husband

Scripture Reading: Titus 2:3-5

Key Verse: Titus 2:4

> Then they can train the younger women to love their husbands and children.

The home, and more specifically the kitchen, is a great setting for what happens in a family. In this "laboratory" you and I have excellent opportunities for loving our husbands and children. In Scripture we see that many events occur around a meal and much is written about the preparation of food. Jesus must have known that people are more willing to listen when one of their basic needs is met, that of food.

Unfortunately, we have sold out to the idea of "fast foods." It's time to get back to the wonderful smells of the home. We can accomplish much when we love our family through our time and efforts at home.

Many years ago the Ball Jar Company issued a serving tray with the following words of wisdom:

How to Preserve a Husband

Be careful in your selection. Do not choose too young. When selected, give your entire thoughts to preparation for domestic use. Some wives insist upon keeping them in a pickle, others are constantly getting them into hot water. This may make them sour, hard, and sometimes bitter. Even poor varieties may be made sweet, tender, and good by garnishing them with patience, well sweetened with love and seasoned with kisses. Wrap them in a mantle of charity. Keep warm with a steady fire of domestic devotion and serve with peaches and cream. Thus prepared, they will keep for years.

Yes, this writer not only knew how to select and prepare good fruit and vegetables, but she also was wise enough to know how to preserve that husband. Oh, if we too could learn to manage our homes so beautifully.

Thoughts for Action

❦ Prepare a new recipe for dinner. Set the table with your finest dishes, light a candle, and dim the lights. Spruce yourself up with a dress, run a brush through your hair, dash on a little perfume, and freshen your makeup. Invite the children to go along with the evening and have them come to the table with their best manners.

❦ Write out in your journal a contract binding you to several actions that will make you a better wife and mother. Be sure to sign it.

❦ Buy one new cookbook that has recipes to fit your family's palate. Plan at least one new recipe each week. If it's good, use it again in the near future.

Additional Scripture Reading

1 Timothy 2:9-15   Proverbs 27:15-16
1 Timothy 3:11

A Treasure in Jars of Clay

Scripture Reading: 2 Corinthians 4:7; 6:3-10

Key Verse: 2 Corinthians 4:7

> But we have this treasure in jars of clay to show that this all-surpassing power is from God and not from us.

When our son, Brad, was in high school he really enjoyed taking courses in ceramics. Even though I am his mother, I can say he was very good. In fact, many of his prized vases, jars, and pots still adorn our home. Brad loved working in clay. When I looked at a lump of reddish tan clay, I was always amazed that Brad was able to make a beautiful vessel out of it. When he added color and a glaze, it became a masterpiece.

In today's Scripture we read that we are "jars of clay." We have a great treasure in us, and this all-surpassing power is from God and not from us.

We live in a world that tells us that if we are righteous enough we can become little gods. However, our reading says that we (Christians) are jars of clay with this great treasure (Jesus Christ) in us. I can go to any nursery in our area and purchase an inexpensive clay pot. They're not of much value. On the other hand my dictionary defines "treasure" as wealth or riches, valuable things. Isn't it amazing we hide our treasures in vaults or safe deposit boxes, but God trusts His treasure in a common clay pot? The only value our clay pot has is in the treasure inside.

I am continually amazed how God can use me, just an ordinary person who is willing to be used for Christ's sake. Basic Christianity is simply stated as Jesus Christ, the treasure, in a clay pot, the Christian. If that is true, and I believe it to be true, then I want to share that valuable treasure inside of me with others.

We need to show others that this all-surpassing power is from God and not from us. Philippians 4:13 states, "I can do everything through him who gives me strength." Can you trust God today to believe that you, a clay pot with a great treasure inside, can do all things because Christ Jesus has given you the strength and power to do it? If we, as women, could believe this promise, we would change ourselves, our families, our churches, our cities, our country, and the world. Trust God today for this belief.

Thoughts for Action

🎔 Jot down in your journal three very large problems facing you. Beside each one state what needs to be done to solve the problem; also write down the date when you want the problem solved.

🎔 Pray specifically for the answer to these problems, remembering the treasure, the strength, living within each of us.

🎔 Give God, in prayer or public testimony, the credit for these answers.

Additional Scripture Reading

Matthew 10:28,39   John 17:20

Asking the Right Questions

Scripture Reading: Romans 8:28-39

Key Verse: Romans 8:28

> *And we know that in all things God works for the good of those who love him, who have been called according to his purpose.*

In doing radio and TV interviews across America and Canada, I have an opportunity to answer a lot of questions. In my earlier days of ministry, I would just immediately answer the interviewer's questions, assuming I knew exactly what he or she meant. In many cases, I answered the wrong question. Bob would very gently instruct me by saying, "Emilie, you need to ask one more question *before* you answer the question." I started to do that. I know now I'm better able to answer the proper question, and I find my interviews go much more smoothly. There is also definitely clearer communication with my audience.

In our passage for today, Paul asks some very strong questions that need to be answered from the proper perspective. It is one thing to ask a good question, but getting the right answer is extremely important.

Let's take a look at the questions and the answers that were mentioned in today's reading.

1. "What, then, shall we say in response to this?" (verse 29).

Answer: In today's passage Paul writes one of the great promises in the New Testament: "And we know that in all things God works for the good of those who love him, who have been called according to his purpose" (verse 28).

- God foreknew us.

- God predestined us to be conformed to the likeness of His son.

- God called us.

- God justified us.

- God glorified us.

What, then, shall we say in response to this? I'm overwhelmed that we have such a marvelous God, one who would do all this for me.

2. "If God is for us, who can be against us?" (verse 31).
Answer: If I know God, nothing, absolutely nothing, can be taken from me that has any value. We have everything in God through His son Jesus.

3. "He who did not spare his own Son, but gave him up for us all—how will he not also, along with him, graciously give us all things?" (verse 32).
Answer: The blessed answer is that He will graciously give us all things according to His will for our lives. What an assurance to know that what we have has been screened by our heavenly Father.

4. "Who will bring charges against those whom God has chosen?" (verse 33).
Answer: No one—absolutely no one.

5. "Who is he that condemns?" (verse 34).
Answer: No one. Jesus Christ is at the right hand of God and is also interceding for us.

6. "Who shall separate us from the love of Christ?" (verse 35).

Answer: No one.

- Neither death nor life
- Neither angels nor demons
- Neither the present nor the future
- Neither height nor depth
- Nor powers
- Nor anything else in all creation

Nothing will be able to separate us from the love of God that is in Christ Jesus our Lord. We can be assured that our questions will be properly answered in Scripture. Try not to rely on the answers of the world, but go to Scripture to get the best answers. And be assured that all things work for our good if we are called according to His purpose.

Thoughts for Action

🍃 In your journal jot down an answer from today's study that you never knew before.

🍃 In your journal jot down a question that has been rolling around in your head. Go to Scripture and see if you can't find a biblical answer. Talk with a pastor, a Bible study leader, or another mature Christian you respect.

Additional Scripture Reading

2 Timothy 3:16   1 John 1:5–2:2
Colossians 2:9

❑ ❑ ❑

Your Family in Christ

Scripture Reading: Ephesians 3:14-21

Key Verse: Ephesians 3:17-19

> And I pray that you, being rooted and established in love, may have power, together with all the saints, to grasp how wide and long and high and deep is the love of Christ, and to know this love that surpasses knowledge—that you may be filled to the measure of all the fullness of God.

An old European story tells of a traveler in Germany who saw a peculiar sight in a tavern where he had stopped for dinner. After the meal, the tavern owner put a great bowl of soup on the floor and gave a loud whistle. A big dog, a large cat, an old raven, and a very large rat came into the room. They all four went to the dish and, without disturbing each other, ate together. After they had dined, the dog, cat, and rat lay before the fire, while Mr. Raven, in his black coat, hopped around the room. The tavern owner had trained these animals so that not one of them bothered to hurt any of the others. He thought that if a dog, a rat, a cat, and a bird can live happily together, little children, especially brothers and sisters, ought to be able to do the same.

Yes, you would think that harmony could be established in our families, but somehow it escapes us.

In today's passage we find that through Paul's prayer we can learn some basic principles for praying for our own family.

1. *Pray that your family may be rooted and established in love.* Oh, how we need families that really love each other. We see so much evil that originates from the family. Ask God to protect your family from evil and put a big hedge of protection around each member. Continually be on guard for the wolf that tries to enter in and devour members of your family.

2. *Pray that you may have power to grasp how wide and long and high and deep is the love of Christ.* Today there is a lack of commitment, a lack of trust, a lack of love in relationships. Pray that your family may begin to grasp the vastness in Christ's love for them individually and collectively.

3. *Pray that your family may know this love that surpasses knowledge.* We cannot comprehend this love that gives beyond our knowledge. But with a great leap of faith, we believe and live the gospel message first within our own life and then share with our family members this love. There are two things to do with the gospel: one, we believe it; two, we live it.

4. *Pray that you will be filled in measure of all the fullness of God.* Each day that I'm in God's Word, I better understand what the fullness of God is all about. After many years of life, I better understand being filled in measure of God's fullness. And being in His family is so much a part of that fullness. Proverbs 24:3-4 states, "By wisdom a house is built, and through understanding it is established; through knowledge its rooms are filled with rare and beautiful treasures."

I will pray for you and your family, that you may grasp these principles and that your rooms will be filled with rare and beautiful treasures.

*Father God, You know that sometimes we have
tensions in our family and we're not as united as we
should be. I earnestly pray that we are rooted and
established in love, and that we might realize how
wide, how long, how high, and how deep Your love*

is for us. Grant me this supplication for my family. Amen.

Thoughts for Action

❦ Go to each member of your family today and tell them that you love them.

❦ Write or phone a friend who lives out of town and express your love for her.

❦ Do an act out of love for someone today, one that expects no return or personal gain.

Additional Scripture Reading

Ephesians 4:29   James 2:15-17

What a Father!

Scripture Reading: Matthew 7:7-12

Key Verse: Matthew 7:11

> *If you, then, though you are evil, know how to give good gifts to your children, how much more will your Father in heaven give good gifts to those who ask him!*

Last year I had some extra time at the Dallas–Fort Worth Airport waiting for a connecting flight to California, so I decided to purchase a Sunday morning newspaper. While looking through the classified section, I came upon a tribute to a father from a bereaved daughter. As I read this, I commented to myself, "What a father!" Here are some of her thoughts:

> ...Daddy was always there when I needed him and his love was always enough.
>
> If he could, he would have spared me pain, cried my tears to protect all sadness from my eyes. If he could, he would have walked with me everywhere I went to make sure I never chose a wrong turn that might bring me harm or defeat. If he could, he would have shielded my innocence from time, but the time he gave me really wasn't his. He could only watch me grow so he could love me for who I was. But Daddy was a wise man. He knew love couldn't be captured or protected. So he let me take my

chances, he gave me my freedom, he let me fight my own battles. I made mistakes but he was always patient.

He was the most generous and giving man of his own self I have ever known and I hope the legacy he left me will be passed to multitudes of generations.

Thank you, Daddy, for all the times and all the nurturing you have given me. The memories will always be in my mind. Now that there will be no more rainbows for us, I will have to let you go, Daddy, but I will always love you.[9]

This dad certainly reflected great qualities of character, ones that we all could model for our own lives. Yet by looking at our verses for today, we see that our heavenly Father will far exceed the goodness of our earthly fathers! Unfortunately, many of us may not have had a pleasant experience with our earthly fathers. In some cases, this has prevented us from being able to trust an unseen heavenly Father.

We certainly have the opportunity to experience the abundance of God if we are willing to ask Him. Your Father in heaven is waiting to give you good gifts if you will ask Him.

Today would be a great time to begin trusting your heavenly Father for all your needs. Go to Him in prayer with thanksgiving, adoration, confession, and petition. He is able to meet you where you are.

> *Father God, I lift up my father and my husband*
> *to You. Please give them the courage to be the men*
> *that You want them to be. May their love abound in*
> *our family. Amen.*

Thoughts for Action

- Write your earthly father a letter expressing your love for him. Don't wait until it is too late.

❦ If your father has passed away, still write that letter in your journal so you can express to him what you have always kept inside.

❦ If your experience with your earthly father wasn't good and you can't write that letter of love, you still might write a letter of hurt and share it with your heavenly Father. Ask Him for the strength to support you while raising your children. Let the pain of the past generation stop in your generation.

❦ If you haven't had a heavenly Father before, open your heart to Jesus today. Know that you have a loving Father who wants to give all things to you.

Additional Scripture Reading

John 3:16	Romans 5:8
John 14:6	John 1:12

The way
each tiny flower
reaches up to heaven
with trust,
we, too, should lift
our hearts to God
and know He cares
for us.

Behavior at the Table

Scripture Reading: Deuteronomy 6:1-9

Key Verse: Deuteronomy 6:6-7

These commandments that I give you today are to be upon your hearts. Impress them on your children. Talk about them when you sit at home and when you walk along the road, when you lie down and when you get up.

Raising children with manners seems to be a lost art. The drive-through window at our favorite fast-food restaurant has dramatically affected how our children eat their food. I see a lot of kids using their fingers in the back of a mini-van, licking their hands when the sauce leaks from the fat of the hamburger. They are usually five minutes late to some activity, somewhere.

Whatever happened to sitting down to the dinner table as a family? To evenings with healthy, nutritious foods, with the TV off and with the conversation centering on what happened during the day in each of our lives? Does this sound foreign to your family? Are you saying, "Please, get real. We are living in the twenty-first century. It's not like it used to be"?

Well, if you stand amazed at what I've said, can you imagine how startled the early Shaker settlers would be if they visited in our homes for an evening? While in Ohio doing a seminar last year, I was privileged to visit one of the restorations of an early Shaker village. In the bookstore I saw an early set of rules framed as a picture that gave advice to children on behavior at the table.

As I read this, I was convicted by how far we have deviated from our early beginnings. May we somehow become challenged to reknow the zeal of the training of our children. In our Scripture passage for today, we see that instructions from the Lord are to be upon our hearts, and that we are to impress them upon our children and talk about them when we walk along the road, when we lie down, and when we get up.

Be committed to properly train your children in *all* areas of life.

Advice to Children on Behavior at the Table

First, in the morning, when you rise,
Give thanks to God, who well supplies
Our various wants, and gives us food,
Wholesome, nutritious, sweet, and good.
Then to some proper place repair,
And wash your hands and face with care;
And ne'er the table once disgrace
With dirty hands or dirty face.
When to your meals you have the call,
Promptly attend, both great and small;
Then kneel and pray, with closed eyes,
That God will bless these rich supplies.
When at the table you sit down,
Sit straight and trim, nor laugh nor frown;
Then let the elder first begin,
And all unite, and follow him.
Of bread, then take a decent piece,
Nor splash about the fat and grease;
But cut your meat both neat and square,
And take of both an equal share.
Also, of bones you'll take your due,
For bones and meat together grew.
If, from some incapacity,

With fat your stomach don't agree,
Or if you cannot pick a bone,
You'll please to let them both alone.
Potatoes, cabbage, turnip, beet,
And every kind of thing you eat,
Must neatly on your plate be laid,
Before you eat with pliant blade;
Nor ever—'tis an awkward matter,
To eat or sip out of the platter.
If bread and butter be your fare,
Or biscuit, and you find there are
Pieces enough, then take your slice,
And spread it over, thin and nice,
On one side, only; then you may
Eat in a decent, comely way.
Yet butter you must never spread
On nut-cake, pie, or dier-bread;
Or bread with milk, or bread with meat,
Butter with these you may not eat.
These things are all the best of food,
And need not butter to be good.
When bread or pie you cut or break,
Touch only what you mean to take;
And have no prints of fingers seen
On that that's left—nay, if they're clean.
Be careful, when you take a sip
Of liquid, don't extend your lip
So far that one may fairly think
That cup and all you mean to drink.
Then clean your knife—don't lick it, pray;
It is a nasty, shameful way—
But wipe it on a piece of bread,
Which snugly by your plate is laid.
Thus clean your knife, before you pass
It into plum or apple-sauce,
Or butter, which you must cut nice,
Both square and true as polish'd dice.

Cut not a pickle with a blade
Whose side with grease is overlaid;
And always take your equal share
Of coarse as well as luscious fare.
Don't pick your teeth, or ears, or nose,
Nor scratch your head, nor tonk your toes;
Nor belch nor sniff, nor jest nor pun,
Nor have the least of play or fun.
If you're oblig'd to cough or sneeze,
Your handkerchief you'll quickly seize,
And timely shun the foul disgrace
Of splattering either food or face.
Drink neither water, cider, beer,
With greasy lip or mucus tear;
Nor fill your mouth with food, and then
Drink, least you blow it out again.
And when you've finish'd your repast,
Clean plate, knife, fork—then, at the last,
Upon your plate lay knife and fork,
And pile your bones of beef and pork:
But if no plate, you may as well
Lay knife and fork both parallel.
Pick up your crumbs, and, where you eat,
Keep all things decent, clean, and neat;
Then rise, and kneel in thankfulness
To Him who does your portion bless;
Then straightly from the table walk,
Nor stop to handle things, nor talk.
If we mean never to offend,
To every gift we must attend,
Respecting meetings, work, or food,
And doing all things as we should.
Thus joy and comfort we shall find,
Love, quietness, and peace of mind;
Pure heavenly Union will increase,
And every evil work will cease.

(Reproduced from the original in the Shaker Collection)

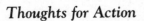

Thoughts for Action

Identify two or three areas of your training that need emphasis. Write in your journal how you plan to concentrate on these areas. Think of several activities that will give you an opportunity to strengthen a deficiency. For example, plan an evening meal where the whole family will sit down at the table and partake in home-prepared food. Depending on the age of your family members, you might delegate...

- help in selecting the menus

- help in shopping for the food

- help in preparing the food

- help in setting the table

- help in providing the centerpiece

- help in serving the food

- help in removing the dishes when the family is finished eating

- help in cleaning the dishes

- help in developing questions that the whole family could talk about (Try this one: "What is the best thing that happened to you today?")

Additional Scripture Reading

Proverbs 22:6   Proverbs 1:1-7
Luke 12:22-34

Create in Me
a New Heart

Scripture Reading: Ezekiel 36:24-27

Key Verse: Ezekiel 36:26a
I will give you a new heart and put a new spirit in you.

As you begin to meet with God and spend time with Him regularly, you will realize that, with your old heart, you can't do what is necessary to make you a godly person. In fact, none of us can make that transformation happen under our own power—and, fortunately, we don't have to. In Ezekiel 36:26, God says, "I will give you a new heart and put a new spirit in you." God offers us a heart transplant, one that is even more remarkable than a medical transplant of a physical heart.

Thankfully, not every one of us will need a new physical heart, but each of us does need a new spiritual heart. Why? Because we are born with a sinful nature. King David acknowledges that fact in the psalms: "Behold, I was brought forth in iniquity, and in sin my mother conceived me" (51:5). The prophet Jeremiah writes: "The heart is deceitful above all things and beyond cure" (Jeremiah 17:9). Jesus teaches that same lesson: "Out of the heart come evil thoughts, murders, adulteries, fornications, thefts, false witness, slanders" (Matthew 15:19). The apostle Paul wrestles with his sin nature:

"For the good that I wish, I do not do; but I practice the very evil that I do not wish. But if I am doing the very thing I do not wish, I am no longer the one doing it, but sin which dwells in me" (Romans 7:19-20). And the apostle John is very direct in his statement about sin: "If we say that we have no sin, we are deceiving ourselves, and the truth is not in us" (1 John 1:8).

So what are we to do? Not even the most skilled physician can cure a sinful heart or give us a new and pure one. But God can and, according to His promise, will. In *Seeing Yourself Through God's Eyes*, June Hunt talks about this process:

> Slowly, after this divine transplant, healing begins and, as promised, your new heart becomes capable of perfect love. Your self-centeredness is now Christ-centeredness. There is healing to replace the hatred; there is a balm for the bitterness. You can face the world with a freedom and a future you have never known before.
>
> "Create in me a clean heart, O God, and renew a steadfast spirit within me" (Psalms 51:10). Once you have a changed heart, you have a changed life. You can love the unlovable, be kind to the unkind, and forgive the unforgivable. All this because you have a new heart—you have God's heart![10]

This kind of heart operation, at the loving hands of your divine Physician, doesn't require major medical insurance. There are no disclaimers or deductibles. God offers this transformation to us free of charge. It costs Him greatly—He gave His only Son for our salvation—but it's a gift to us. All we have to do is accept it—no strings attached.

Father God, You know that I need a new heart—not one that a doctor transplants but one

You change. Give me that newness of spirit that refreshes like the spring water which flows through the valley. Amen.

Thoughts for Action

❦ Pray to God in earnest that you truly want a new heart.

❦ In your journal write down five areas of your life where you want to create a new heart and spirit.

❦ Under each of the areas write down two to three activities you will do to accomplish these changes. Beside each activity write a date when you will accomplish each.

Additional Scripture Reading

2 Corinthians 5:17   Romans 5:5

Commit to God and to Your Spouse

Scripture Reading: Ephesians 5:15-21

Key Verse: Ephesians 5:21
Submit to one another out of reverence for Christ.

You've probably never heard of Nicolai Pestretsov, but now you may never forget him. He was 36 years old, a sergeant major in the Russian army, stationed in Angola. His wife had traveled the long distance from home to visit him when, on an August day, South African military units entered the country in quest of black nationalist guerrillas taking sanctuary there. When the South Africans encountered the Russian soldiers, four people were killed and the rest of the Russians fled—except for Sergeant Major Pestretsov.

The South African troops captured Pestretsov, and a military communique explained the situation: "Sergeant Major Nicolai Pestretsov refused to leave the body of his slain wife, who was killed in the assault on the village. He went to the body of his wife and would not leave it, although she was dead."

What a picture of commitment—and what a series of questions it raises! Robert Fulghum, who tells this story, asks these questions:

Why didn't he run and save his own hide?
What made him go back? Is it possible that he
loved her? Is it possible that he wanted to hold
her in his arms one last time? Is it possible that
he needed to cry and grieve? Is it possible that he
felt the stupidity of war? Is it possible that he felt
the injustice of fate? Is it possible that he thought
of children, born or unborn? Is it possible that
he didn't care what became of him now? Is it
possible? We don't know. Or at least we don't
know for certain. But we can guess. His actions
answer. [11]

What do your actions say about your commitment to your
husband? What do your attitudes and your words reveal?
Standing by the commitment you made to your spouse—the
commitment you made before God and many witnesses—is
key to standing by your man.

Picture again Sergeant Major Pestretsov kneeling by the
side of his wife's lifeless body, not wanting to leave the woman
to whom he'd pledged his life even when his very life was at
stake. That is a high level of commitment. We are to be as
committed. We who are married are to be as committed to our
spouse as Christ is to the church He died for. In fact, as Christians, our marriages are to be a witness to the world of Christ's
love and grace. Clearly, marriage is not to be entered into
casually.

In light of the importance God places on marriage, Bob
and I take the premarital counseling we do very seriously. We
never, for instance, encourage two people to get married if one
is a Christian and the other is not (2 Corinthians 6:14). A
marriage needs to be rooted in each partner's commitment to
love and serve the Lord, or else the union will be divided from
the start. In addition, only a Christian marriage will result in
a Christian home, a home which glorifies God and acts as His
witness to the world.

I can vividly remember an evening Bob and I were sitting on the couch in my living room. He cupped my face in his hands and said, "Emilie, I love you, but I can't ask you to marry me." I was stunned. I couldn't understand why two people who were in love couldn't get married.

As Bob looked steadfastly into my eyes, I asked, "Why not?" With all the courage he could muster, Bob answered firmly but gently, "Because you are not a Christian." Very innocently I asked Bob, "How do I become a Christian?" From that moment I began to consider whether Jesus might actually be the Messiah my Jewish people had long waited for.

After several months of seeking answers, I prayed one evening at my bedside, "Dear God, if You have a Son and if Your Son is Jesus our Messiah, please reveal Him to me!" I expected a voice to answer immediately, but God waited a few weeks to reveal Himself to me. Then, one Sunday morning, I responded to my pastor's challenge to accept Jesus Christ as my personal Savior, and that evening I was baptized.

Being obedient to God has meant being blessed by a rich and wonderful marriage that is rooted in His love and dedicated to Him. Furthermore, vowing before God to love Bob through the good times and the bad has reinforced my commitment to him when the times were indeed bad. Had my vows been to Bob alone, they might have been easier to walk away from. But God's witness of our vows and the foundation He gives to Christian couples enables us to stand together whatever comes our way.

> Lord, what joy that we may tell other people
> that it works.
>
> —Corrie ten Boom

Father God, it's sometimes difficult to stand by the commitment I've made to my spouse. We all want to do our own thing our own way. Help me to

stay true to the vow I made before You and other witnesses. I truly want to commit to You and to my husband, and to receive the blessings that You promise in
Scripture when we do just that. Amen.

Thoughts for Action

❦ Today in your journal write down a fresh, new commitment to your God and to your spouse.

❦ Make a commitment to be willing to "submit to one an
other" in all things (Ephesians 5:21).

❦ Touch your marriage ring (if you wear one). Think back to
your wedding day and review your wedding vows. Touch
your ring regularly and each time think about those vows.

Additional Scripture Reading

Ephesians 5:22-33   Ephesians 6:10-18

The Spirit of a Woman

Scripture Reading: 1 Peter 3:3-6

Key Verse: 1 Peter 3:4

> [Your beauty] should be that of your inner self, the
> unfading beauty of a gentle and quiet spirit, which is
> of great worth in God's sight.

Oh, if only we could truly capture the spirit of today's passage! Today we are drastically in need of women who are satisfied with themselves inwardly and reflect a soft and tender
peacefulness in their lives. Too often as women we have
become loud, aggressive, and masculine in manners. We have
left God's pattern of womanhood, sometimes trying to be better men than men themselves.

How do I define "feminine"? Not by a particular style of
dress or interior decorating. "Feminine" can take on an infi-
nite variety of physical appearances. Instead, I see "feminine"
as a softness, a gentleness, and a graciousness. That's not to
say, though, that a woman cannot be the president of a corporation or an active participant in the business world. She
certainly can, yet a feminine woman will have a softness and
graciousness that men simply don't have. To me, "feminine"
also means that a woman has a sense of who she is apart from
what she does. She nurtures a strong spirituality and manifests
the fruit of the Spirit in every aspect of her life (Galatians
5:22-23). "Femininity" also brings to my mind a woman's deep

concern for her husband and children, the ability to submit to her husband when appropriate (Ephesians 5:21), and the maternal awareness that she is raising not only her children but generations to come. Finally, a truly feminine woman understands the "mystique" of being a godly wife and mother.

The "gentle and quiet spirit" which Peter refers to—this tranquillity, this sense that a woman is at peace with herself, this ability to share the fruit of the Spirit with people she comes in contact with—results from a woman's relationship with God. When a woman has this inner peace, she doesn't feel any need to prove herself to her husband or to anyone else. Confident in herself and aware of her God-given strengths, she doesn't feel compelled to use those strengths to control other people. She enjoys an inner contentment that isn't based on accomplishments, status, authority, power, or other people's opinions.

As I mentioned earlier, this woman of God has learned the value of *being* as opposed to *doing*. Too many women today have forgotten how to simply *be*. They have bought into the lie of doing and have become highly obsessive-compulsive about getting work done. As a result, they are cut off from their feminine feelings and nature.

A woman who walks closely with her God, however, is free from competitiveness, aggressiveness, and the need to prove her worth. Yes, she may be aggressive and high-energy by temperament or competitive and very capable in the business world, but the fact is that she is affirmed not by other people but by her God. Such a woman "speaks with wisdom, and faithful instruction is on her tongue" (Proverbs 31:26), and her family is blessed: "Her husband has full confidence in her and lacks nothing of value. She brings him good, not harm, all the days of her life....Her children arise up and call her blessed" (Proverbs 31:11-12,28). Such a woman inspires the man of her life to rise to his own greatness, and she supports him unconditionally in his search for fulfillment and achievement. And such a woman—one closely in tune with God—is indeed worthy of praise as she models godly values and high moral standards. A woman's gentle and quiet spirit makes her a blessing to the people around her.

Gentleness, patience, and devotion to God—traits which I view as components of godly femininity—are qualities which hold society together and provide hope for the future. We have an incredible responsibility! History shows that as the woman goes, so goes the family. You give meaning and purpose to a home. You are the heartbeat, pumping vital blood into the family system by setting the spirit and tone. You help others establish and live by moral standards.

The femininity I am describing teaches, inspires, and civilizes. It brings glory to God and hope to His world. And such femininity also has a real "mystique" about it. Men look to women to bring out their gentler natures and their highest ideals, to inflame their passions, and to motivate them to achievement.

One mother, wise about the more practical side of the feminine mystique, offered a piece of advice to her future daughter-in-law. The groom-to-be was a minister and an avid reader who spent large amounts of time in the library studying and preparing for the next Sunday's sermon. The mother said to her son's intended: "John loves to study and often works late into the night at the library. Don't try to change him, but always have his dinner in a warm oven and keep a pot of coffee on the stove." The young lady listened to her future mother-in-law and, at last account, she had been married to Pastor John for over 40 years.

Pastor John's wife was an example of "that kind of deep beauty...seen in the saintly women of old who trusted God and fitted in with her husband's plans" (1 Peter 3:5 TLB). This type of woman can be irresistible to men. This femininity is a rarity in today's culture, and the traditional male still seeks valiantly for it. The mystique works. Are you letting it enrich your marriage?

Thoughts for Action

❦ Write in your journal several activities that help you feel feminine. Consider a few of these:

—Buy some fresh flowers for your home. (Silk flowers will do, too.)

—Light a candle or small oil lamp by the kitchen sink, the nightstand, or the bathtub.

—Get a new haircut or add something new to your makeup collection.

—Read a love story or poem.

—Buy that lacy dress you've been looking at for the last month.

—Pamper yourself with a new bottle of perfume.

—Buy a new set of sheets—the kind with soft ruffles on the edges.

—Start a daily exercise program. (If you don't have access to a gym or aerobics on videotape, walk!)

—Unclutter your bedroom. Reserve it for sleep and romance.

❦ Choose at least one new activity this week and then another one next week.

Additional Scripture Reading

Matthew 6:33   Ephesians 4:32

Her Children Call Her Blessed

Scripture Reading: Proverbs 31

Key Verse: Proverbs 31:28a
Her children arise and call her blessed.

Consider Sarah Edwards, the wife of theologian and preacher Jonathan Edwards and the mother of 11 children. According to one biographer, Sarah's children and her children's children through the generations were a tribute to this woman in their distinguished positions as college presidents, professors, attorneys, judges, physicians, senators, governors, and even a vice president of the United States! What influenced 1400 of Sarah Edwards's descendants to become such fine citizens? One author suggests that Sarah treated her children with patience, courtesy, respect, and love. Being a deeply Christian woman, she taught her children to work and deal with what life brought their way according to biblical principles. Convinced that until children can obey their parents they will never be obedient to God, Sarah was also a firm disciplinarian. But she never resorted to words of anger. Her home emanated love and harmony. And what were the results of her efforts as homemaker and mother?

As [biographer] Elizabeth Dodds makes abundantly clear in her book, a mother is not merely rearing her one generation of children.

145

She is also affecting future generations for good or ill. All the love, nurture, education, and character-building that spring from Mother's work influence those sons and daughters. The results show up in the children's accomplishments, attitudes toward life and parenting capacity. For example, one of Sarah Edwards' grandsons, Timothy Dwight, president of Yale (echoing Lincoln) said, "All that I am and all that I shall be, I owe to my mother."[12]

Have you ever felt discontent in your role as wife and mother, as though what you do makes very little difference? I think we all have. But consider this:

As one ponders this praise [by Timothy Dwight], the question arises: Are we women unhappy in our mothering and wife role because we make too little, rather than too much of that role? Do we see what we have to give our husbands and children as minor rather than major, and consequently send them into the world without a healthy core identity and strong spiritual values? [13]

Are you fulfilled in your role as wife and mother? Do you have purpose? Fulfillment and the peace it offers don't come free. You will work and sacrifice as you live out your purpose and find fulfillment as a woman of God, a wife, and a mother.

Sarah Edwards spent many hours serving her husband and children. Her responsibilities were many and the demands on her great, yet she seemed to offer her family a sense of serenity as she cared for them. And despite how different our world is today, I believe a wife and mother can still make her home a place of serenity, a place where her children will rise up and bless her. It starts when she herself discovers and nurtures a serenity that God alone gives.

> *Father God, how I want my children to arise and call me blessed! Children today so often criticize and put down their mothers. I so want my children to be different. Give me the wisdom and strength to discern attitudes and behaviors in me which will place in my children's hearts the desire to call me blessed. Amen.*

Thoughts for Action

❦ Here are some ways to develop a serenity that will weather the demands of being a wife and mother:

—Sit in a quiet room for 5, 10, or 15 minutes and reflect on what God is doing in your life.

—Wait upon the Lord. Listen for Him to direct, encourage, guide, and teach.

—Just sit and hold hands with your husband and think about God's love, power, and peace.

—Turn on some peaceful music. Avoid loud sounds and high volume.

—Take a walk—at the beach, on a mountain trail, in a snowy meadow. Ski down a hill or watch the leaves fall off the trees.

—Take a warm bubble bath.

—Draw a picture.

—Find a new hobby.

—Eliminate some of the confusion in your life.

—Don't drive over the speed limit.

—Ride a bicycle instead of driving a car.

—Feed the ducks in the park.

—Tell your husband that you love him.

- Write in your journal several activities that help you feel serene.
- Do at least one of these activities this week and then another one next week.

Additional Scripture Reading

Genesis 2:18-24 Luke 1:39-49

Little Jelly Beans

Scripture Reading: John 3:16-21

Key Verse: John 3:16

> *For God so loved the world that he gave his one and only Son, that whoever believes in him shall not perish but have eternal life.*

A friend placed a simple little bag of colored jelly beans in my hand. A card was attached to the bag. In passing I thought, "Cute gift." Placing the bag on the table with a quick thank you, I went on to visit with my friend.

It was actually several days later when I picked up the small package of colored jelly beans to throw a few into my mouth. However, in order to get to those silly beans I had to cut the attached card off. In so doing I noticed the words on the card. Here is what they said:

Little Jelly Beans

Little jelly beans
Tell a story true
A tale of Father's love
Just for me and you.

GREEN is for the waving palms
BLUE for the skies above

149

BROWN for the soft earth where
People sat hearing of His love.

A SPECKLED bean for fish and sand
RED for precious wine
And BLACK is for the sin He washed
From your soul and mine.

PURPLE'S for the sadness of
His family and friends,
And WHITE is for the glory of the
Day He rose again.

Now you've heard the story
You know what each color means
The story of our Father's love
Told by some jelly beans.

So every morning take a bean
They're really very yummy
Something for the soul, you see.
And something for the tummy.

It's been a year since that gift of jelly beans was put into my hand. I have not eaten them—they sit on my desk as a beautiful reminder of what God has done and given to me. When I see those jelly beans I remember to thank our Lord for the earth and sky, for friends and family, for a family of God that is so big and mighty, for the love and prayers of others. And most of all, for our heavenly Father's love, the love gift of His very own Son, Jesus Christ.

*Father God, thank You for the simple reminders
of who You are and what You have done. You are a
great and awesome God. Help me to remember that
always. Amen.*

Thoughts for Action

 Thank the Lord today for the beautiful world He created.

 Meditate on our key verse, John 3:16.

 What does that verse mean to you?

Additional Scripture Reading

    John 5:24   John 10:28

The True Christmas Spirit

Scripture Reading: Matthew 7:7-12

Key Verse: Matthew 7:12

> So in everything, do to others what you would have them do to you, for this sums up the Law and the Prophets.

Edwin Markham wrote a poem based on a story by Tolstoy that beautifully illustrates how we may demonstrate the true Christmas spirit.

One night Conrad, a cobbler of shoes, dreamed that Christ would come to his shop on the following day. Early the next morning Conrad went to the woods to gather greens and flowers to decorate his simple shop for the Lord's coming.

All morning he waited, but the only visitor was an old man who asked if he might sit down to rest. Conrad saw that his shoes were worn. Before sending the stranger on his way, Conrad put the best pair of shoes in the shop on the old man's feet.

Throughout the afternoon Conrad waited for the Lord's coming, but the only person he saw was an old woman struggling under a heavy load. Out of compassion he brought her in and gave her some of the food he had prepared for Christ. She went on her way refreshed.

Just as evening was falling, a lost child entered Conrad's shop. Conrad carried the child home, and then hurried back, lest he miss the coming of Christ.

Though Conrad waited long and patiently, Christ did not come. Finally, in disappointment, the old cobbler cried:

> "Why is it, Lord, that your feet delay?
> Did You forget that this was the day?"
> Then soft in the silence a voice he heard:
> "Lift up your heart, for I kept my word.
> Three times I came to your friendly door;
> Three times my shadow was on your floor.
> I was the beggar with the bruised feet;
> I was the woman you gave to eat;
> I was the child on the homeless street!"

May you, dear reader, know the true meaning of Christmas. May you know Jesus Christ as your Savior, and may you find the joy of sharing with others in need. Then Christmas for you will not merely be a holiday, but a holy day, a celebration of the love of God and love for others. And that is what Christmas is really all about.

Thoughts for Action

What are some things we can do to help others when holidays come? Start with my list and add some of your ideas to it.

- Take food—homemade if possible—to those who may not have extra.

- Decorate the home of a family who can't afford decorations this year.

- Clean someone's house or fix their car.

❦ Offer your babysitting services free of charge to a single parent.

Additional Scripture Reading

Galatians 6:9   Colossians 3:17
2 Thessalonians 3:13   Ephesians 6:7-8

The Two Shall Become One

Scripture Reading: Genesis 2:20a-25

Key Verse: Genesis 2:24

> *For this reason a man will leave his father and mother and be united to his wife, and they will become one flesh.*

One of Aesop's fables tells the story of a wise father who sensed disharmony among his sons and decided to bring them together to discuss this strife. He told each of his four sons to bring a twig to the meeting.

As the young men assembled, the father took each boy's twig and easily snapped it in half. Then he gathered four twigs, tied them together in a bundle, and asked each son to try to break the bundle. Each one tried to no avail. The bundle would not snap.

After each son had tried valiantly to break the bundle, the father asked his boys what they had learned from the demonstration. The oldest son said, "If we are individuals, anyone can break us, but if we stick together, no one can harm us." The father said, "You are right. You must always stand together and be strong."

What is true for the four brothers is equally true for a husband and wife. If we don't stand together and let God make us one in spite of our differences, we will easily be defeated.

As I studied today's Scripture passage, I saw God calling a husband and wife to:

- *departure* ("A man shall leave his father and mother...")
- *permanence* ("And shall cleave to his wife...")
- *oneness* ("And they shall become one flesh")

All three steps must be taken if a marriage is to stand strong.

In God's sight, we become one at the altar when we say our vows to one another before Him. But practically speaking, oneness between a husband and wife is a process that happens over a period of time, over a lifetime together.

Becoming one with another person can be a very difficult process. It isn't easy to change from being independent and self-centered to sharing every aspect of your life and self with another person. The difficulty is often intensified when you're older and more set in your ways when you marry or, as was the case for Bob and me, when the two partners come from very different family, religious, or financial backgrounds. I, for instance, came from an alcoholic family and was raised by a verbally and physically abusive father. Bob came from a warm, loving family where yelling and screaming simply didn't happen. It took us only a few moments to say our vows and enter into oneness in God's eyes, but we have spent nearly 50 years blending our lives and building the oneness which we enjoy today.

Becoming one doesn't mean becoming the same, however. Oneness means sharing the same degree of commitment to the Lord and to the marriage, the same goals and dreams, and the same mission in life. Oneness is internal conformity to one another, not an external conformity. It's not the Marines with their short haircuts, shiny shoes, straight backs, and characteristic walk. The oneness and internal conformity of a marriage relationship comes with the unselfish act of allowing

God to shape us into the marriage partner He would have us be. Oneness results when two individuals reflect the same Christ. Such spiritual oneness produces tremendous strength and unity in a marriage and in the family.

The two marriage partners must leave their families and let God make them one. Men help the cleaving happen when they show—not just tell—their wives that they are the most important priority after God. Likewise, a wife needs to let her husband know how important he is to her. Your man cannot be competing with your father or any other male for the number-one position in your life. He must know that you respect, honor, and love him if he is to act out his proper role as husband confidently. Your clear communication of your love for him will strengthen the bond of marriage.

Consider what Paul writes to the church at Philippi: "Make my joy complete by being of the same mind, maintaining the same love, united in spirit, intent on one purpose" (Philippians 2:2). This verse has guided me as I worked to unite my family in purpose, thought, and deed. After many years of trial, error, and endless hours of searching, I can say that we are truly united in our purpose and direction. If you were to ask Bob to state our purpose and direction, his answer would match mine: Matthew 6:33—"Seek first his kingdom and his righteousness, and all these things will be given to you." As we have faced decisions through the years, we have asked ourselves, "Are we seeking God's kingdom and His righteousness?" Will doing this help us find His kingdom and experience His righteousness? Or are we seeking our own edification or our own satisfaction? We both hold to this standard whenever we have to decide an issue, and that oneness of purpose helps make our marriage work.

Larry Crabb points out another important dimension to the oneness of a husband and wife when he writes, "The goal of oneness can be almost frightening when we realize that God does not intend [only] that my wife and I find our personal needs met in marriage. He also wants our relationship to validate the claims of Christianity to a watching world as an example of the power of Christ's redeeming love to overcome the divisive effects of sin." [14]

The world does not value permanence and oneness in a marriage, and much of our culture works to undermine those characteristics. But knowing what God intends marriage to be, working to leave, cleave, and become one with our spouse, will help us shine God's light in a very dark world.

> *Father God, today's reading has made me aware that there are several areas in my life where my husband and I need better unity. Please give me a proper sensitivity to these areas when I approach him. You know that I want total oneness in purpose of spirit. I thank You now for what You are going to do in this situation. Amen.*

Thoughts for Action

- Set a date with your mate and write down five things you agree on regarding family, discipline, manners, values, church, home, etc.

- At the same session write down several items in which you are not one as yet. State what your differences are regarding each. Discuss these differences. Agree to pray about these differences. Set an appointment for your next date to again discuss these items.

- Ways to say "I Love You":

    —Deliver something in a heart-shaped box, be it jelly beans, chocolates, or jewelry.

    —Give a certificate for a massage, facial, or a weekend getaway.

—Have firewood delivered, then deliver yourself and refreshments.

Additional Scripture Reading

Philippians 2:2   Matthew 19:3-6

Three Loves

Scripture Reading: Deuteronomy 6:4-9

Key Verse: Deuteronomy 6:5
Love the Lord your God with all your heart and with all your soul and with all your strength.

Today's Scripture talks about three basic loves:

- Love for God
- Love for your neighbor
- Love for yourself

Our circle of love is full when we are able to love in this way. The whole world would know of Jesus if the Christians in the church would manifest these three basic love relationships. Our passage challenges us by giving a directive to:

- Put these commandments in our hearts.
- Impress them on our children.
- Talk about them continually.
- Tie them as symbols on our bodies.
- Write them on our door frames and gates.

God must be serious about this because He engulfs our lives with continuous reminders of His commandments to love.

How do we manifest these three loves? Paul, in writing to the church at Ephesus, includes a section on a believer's relationship with the Holy Spirit, beginning in Ephesians 5:18: "Instead, be filled with the Spirit." In the verses that follow we learn that we are to be satisfied with self, God, and others.

If we are satisfied with ourselves, Paul teaches us to manifest it in speaking and singing words of joy: "Speak to one another with psalms, hymns, and spiritual songs. Sing and make music in your heart to the Lord" (verse 19). Satisfied lives will be ones of joy, praise, and excitement. They will reflect positive thoughts, ideas, and praises to God. What a great test to see where our personal satisfaction is! Are we known as a person who is fun to be around or as someone who people avoid? God wants us to be satisfied with ourselves and reflect the joy of the Lord in our soul, mind, and spirit.

Paul continues in verse 20, "Always giving thanks for all things in the name of our Lord Jesus Christ to God, even the Father" (NASB). This verse shows *our satisfaction with God.* If we are satisfied, we find ourselves giving thanks for all things. We have an appreciative heart for all that goes on around us. The positive words flow from our lips unto God.

Our third satisfaction is with other people. In verse 21 Paul teaches, "And be subject to one another in the fear of Christ." As women, we find that when we love God and ourselves, we become equipped to be submissive to others. These words, "subject" or "submissive," unfortunately, have taken a beating in today's culture. In essence, these words are telling us to be satisfied with other people to the point that we are willing to step aside in our personal relationships. We are willing to allow another's needs to take precedence over our own. The submission is to be mutual among Christians, among husband and wife, and based on reverence for God. It is impossible to be subject to one another by human desire. It is possible only when we mutually submit to one another out of respect for God.

Ephesians 5:18-21 truly gives us guidelines for being satisfied with God, with ourselves, and with others.

As I have taught this concept over the years, I have used a diagram to illustrate my point:

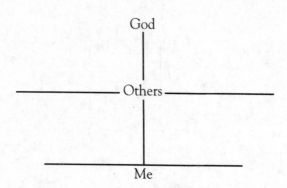

As you can see, we have vertical and horizontal relationships. The vertical relationship is between God and me, and the horizontal relationship is between myself and other people. I find that when God and I have the proper relationship, my relationship with others falls into proper alignment. If I have dissatisfaction with myself and others, I realize that I am not responding to God properly. Over the years, God has taught me to put first things first: to love God, to love self, and to love others.

Father God, life is so difficult at times. There seems to be so many things pulling at me that I get exhausted trying to be all things to all people. Let me start each day concentrating on the three loves. It seems so basic, but I know it takes a lifetime to accomplish. Amen.

Thoughts for Action

❧ In your journal write down several ways you presently express love to:

—God

—Others

—Self

❧ Now write down several new ways to express love in these three areas.

❧ Make or purchase a sign or plaque that states to the world that you are a Christian. Put this sign by your front door. (Make sure you walk your talk and not talk your walk.)

Additional Scripture Reading

Ephesians 5:18-21   Matthew 22:36-40

To Know the Love of Christ

Scripture Reading: Ephesians 3:16-21

Key Verse: Ephesians 3:18b
> ...to grasp how wide and long and high and deep is the love of Christ.

Bob and I are usually not home on Friday evenings, but we were on the night of June 23. We were preparing for a marriage seminar in our home the next morning. After getting everything organized and ready, Bob and I went to the kitchen and began popping popcorn. The phone rang at 9:30 P.M. I remember checking my watch, wondering who would be calling so late to get directions for tomorrow.

After Bob's first few words on the phone, I knew something serious had happened. Our dear friends of 20 years were calling for care, help, support, and prayers. Their son, Jimmy, had been in a terrible car accident on a street near our home. He had hit a palm tree on Victoria Avenue. That's all it took for Bob to say we would be right there.

We had met Jim and Barbara DeLorenzo the first year we moved to Riverside. Jimmy was about 8 years old. They were new Christians, and God truly bonded our hearts and friendship almost immediately. Over the years our families have experienced many memorable times. We still call Jim, Jr. "Jimmy."

But at that moment all we could think of was how dangerous Victoria Avenue is, with palm trees lining both sides of the street and also in a row down the median. The years our children were in high school, eight students had died due to palm tree accidents. We couldn't believe this was happening to Jimmy. He was an excellent driver. He knew very well the danger of Victoria Avenue and how to handle cars in dangerous situations. As we drove to the hospital, all we could do was pray and ask God to spare this child.

The first words that came from Big Jim's mouth when Jim and Barbara met us in emergency was, "Jimmy wasn't driving and the two young men are alive."

The car was going 65 MPH when it lost control on a curve and crashed into a palm tree, literally wrapping itself around the tree. The pictures of the accident later showed that only a miracle of God could explain Jimmy's and his friend's lives being spared. The "jaws of life" were used to cut these young men out of the car, and thankfully drugs and alcohol were immediately ruled out.

Jim and Bob stayed with Jimmy as the doctors stitched up his lacerated head, eyes, and hands. Barbara and I prayed. Rather, I prayed as Barbara cried and shook from shock. We knew the situation was in God's hands. We also knew of other parents who had lost their sons and daughters through similar accidents.

Jimmy is okay today, but only after plastic surgery, a shaved head, hundreds of stitches, and a plastic pin in his eye socket.

As Barbara and Jim reflect on the experience, they see what a precious time of love and friendship occurred. The bond we felt between us will always be there. As Barb says, "It's beyond words, the changes we've made with priorities in our life. The results have been a closer prayer life within the family and such growth of fellowship with God and friends, not to mention the times we've had with our son and his recovery."

Their roots of faith in God's love and protection have deepened. They do realize how wide, how high, and how deep God's love really is.

Yes! So easy to read, but sometimes so very difficult to live out in life.

Thoughts for Action

❦ Write in your journal several incidents or blessings which have happened in your life that reflect God's love for you.

❦ Today be a doer of God's Word and not just a hearer. Go out and unselfishly love someone.

Additional Scripture Reading

Philippians 1:9-11   Colossians 2:2-7

We find God
in so many things,
in flowers wakened
with each Spring,
in butterflies and
sunsets grand,
we see God's love—
we touch God's hand.

Respect Your Husband

Scripture Reading: Ephesians 5:22-33

Key Verse: Ephesians 5:33
> However, each one of you also must love his wife
> as he loves himself, and the wife must respect her
> husband.

How your family functions can reveal a lot about the respect you and your husband have for each other. How you and your husband communicate can also give an indication of the level of respect you show one another. Today we're going to take a look at a woman's respect for her husband.

Jerry and Barbara Cook suggest that wives read the following message to their husbands. Let it be the catalyst for a discussion about your marriage.

> I married a man I respect;
>> I have no need to bow and defer.
> I married a man I adore and admire;
>> I don't need to be handed a list entitled "how to build
>>> his ego" or "the male need for admiration."
> Love, worship, loyalty, trust—these are inside me;
>> They motivate my actions.
>>> To reduce them to rules destroys my motivation.

I choose to serve him, to enjoy him.
We choose to live together and grow together, to stretch
    our capacities for love even when it hurts and looks like
    conflict.
We choose to learn to know each other as real people, as
    two unique individuals unlike any other two.
Our marriage is commitment to love;
    to belong to each other
    to know and understand
    to care
    to share ourselves, our goals,
    interest, desires, needs.
Out of that commitment the actions follow.
Love defines our behavior
    and our ways of living together.
And since we fail to meet not only the demands
    of standards but also the simple requirements of love
We are forced to believe in forgiveness...and grace. [15]

Notice that today's Scripture reading doesn't *suggest* that you respect your husband; it makes a firm statement, "The wife must respect her husband." Our culture says it's okay to give *after* you receive, but God's principles are usually opposite from the world's point-of-view. God says give first, then you will receive. Be a risk-taker in your marriage; don't be afraid to give. God would never tell you to do something that wasn't right and that wouldn't bring blessings in your life.

    God's design for marriage is for husbands to love their wives as Christ loved the church and for wives to respect their husbands. Christ loved the world enough to die for it, and that kind of love is worthy of respect.

    Now consider a passage from H. Norman Wright's *Quiet Times for Couples* in which he addresses the issue of respect more specifically. What does this passage show you about your marriage and the respect you show your husband?

Do you have a respectful marriage? This is part of our calling as believers. [Scripture] instructs both husbands and wives to respond to one another with respect. But do you understand what that means? Respect in marriage means ministering to your partner through listening, a loving embrace, a flexible mind and attitude, and a gracious spirit. It means looking past faults and differences and seeing strengths and similarities. It means sharing concerns mutually instead of attempting to carry the load yourself.

Consider the following questions as you evaluate your respect for one another:

- In a tense situation, do I cut off my partner when he or she holds a view different from mine?

- When I think my partner is wrong, do I become offensive and harsh trying to put him or her in place?

- In trying to get a point across, am I gently persuasive or opinionated and demanding?

- Am I driven so much by the need to be right that I try to pressure my spouse into my position? Do I intimidate my partner?

Yes, these are questions which meddle. But answering them is a good step toward building a respectful marriage. As one author said, respect begins when we "learn to practice careful listening rather than threatened opposition, honest expression rather than resentment, flexibility rather than rigidity, loving censure rather than harsh coercion, encouragement rather than intimidation."

How's the respect in your marriage relationship? [16]

When we show our mate respect in the ways that Norm Wright outlines, we do much to strengthen our marriage. And you, as a wife, have an important opportunity to show your respect for your husband each time he makes a decision, good or bad—and some will be bad. Let me remind you that Babe Ruth struck out more times than any other baseball player, but he also hit 60 home runs in a season. Keep in mind, too, that today's baseball players make millions of dollars for batting .300—and batting .300 means getting on base 300 times out of 1000 times at bat. Looked at differently, that statistic means *not* getting on base 700 times. And still the world is willing to pay greatly for a performance like that! So perhaps we can be a little more forgiving and respectful when our mates make a few bad decisions. When you can do that for your husband, you will be showing him your love in a very powerful way.

You will also be loving your husband with the love of Christ. "When we fail," Norm Wright observes, "and often we do—God keeps no record of it. God does not deal with us according to our sins (Psalm 103:10), but He accepts us in Christ. Because of the work of Jesus on the cross, you are accepted as blameless. [So] perhaps one of your most important callings in marriage is to follow the model of Christ by being a living benediction to your partner. Help keep your mate from stumbling, and when he or she does fall, don't keep track of it. Score keeping isn't a part of marriage; however, forgiveness is."[17]

Encourage your man when he makes decisions. Let go of unrealistic standards of perfection and love him for who he is, a fallible human being. Let your home be a place where he isn't constantly evaluated and where he doesn't have to perform in order to be accepted. Focus on his skills and abilities, and let him lead from his strengths. Finally, don't keep track of the poor decisions he makes. Your husband will become a more confident decision maker and a better leader when he knows that you are in his corner no matter what the outcome.

Accept your husband unconditionally (unless he is doing something in violation of God's commands). Encourage your husband to be the unique person God created him to be. Be a source of serenity in his life and grant him the solitude he needs to dream, to recover, and to be with the Lord. Encourage him to develop friendships with other men and welcome the new perspectives, interests, and passions these friends may introduce into your husband's life.

> *Father God, touch my heart. Help me to respect my husband unconditionally. Let me risk rejection and reach out to show him that I do respect him in a godly way. May I be obedient to this command. Amen.*

Thoughts for Action

❦ Write in your journal five expectations you have for your husband.

❦ After each one write, "I release you, and you are free to become the man God wants you to be!"

❦ Also, list in your journal how you are going to respect your husband more.

❦ Leave a surprise love message on his computer or fax machine.

❦ Call your husband every hour one morning or afternoon with one more reason why you respect him.

Additional Scripture Reading

Mark 10:35-45   John 13:1-17

Not on Your Permanent Record

Scripture Reading: Romans 8:1-9

Key Verse: Romans 8:1-2

Therefore, there is now no condemnation for those who are in Christ Jesus, because through Christ Jesus the law of the Spirit of life set me free from the law of sin and death.

One young man we know relates an incident in his life that vividly illustrates the great promise in today's key verse. When he was in the fifth grade, he and a friend rode their bicycles to school each day. School started at 9:00 A.M. and they couldn't get on the playground before 8:30 A.M. One day they had tailwinds which had them arriving to the playground before the appropriate time. Of course, no supervision was available, but did that stop them? No! As boys will do, they went on the playground early. They were having a ball when a teacher arrived and firmly stated, "Boys, go to the principal's office!"

Upon arriving at Mr. Fox's office, they had to sit in the reception area. Just imagine two good boys sitting there waiting for the principal to come out of his big office. They didn't know what was going to happen to them, maybe expulsion, a call to the police, a trip to jail, or a phone call telling parents to come get them. Their knees were shaking and their voices were quivering when Mr. Fox appeared and invited the boys into his office.

After hearing the story, Mr. Fox stood up and very authoritatively stated, "This will go on your permanent record." Our young friend thought he would die. He just *knew* this would probably prevent him from graduating from elementary, junior high, high school, and college, and it would definitely prevent him from becoming a dentist! He also knew that his parents would be very upset.

When he got home that evening, he related the incident to his dad. His dad assured the boy that this event would not prevent him from obtaining his academic endeavor.

Have you ever been crippled because of some sin that you have felt has gone on your permanent record of life? In Romans 8, Paul assures us that there is now no condemnation for those who are in Christ Jesus, because through Christ Jesus the law of the Spirit of life has set us free from the law of sin and death.

The truly godly person never forgets that he was at one time an object of God's holy and just wrath. He never forgets that Christ Jesus came into the world to save sinners, and the godly person feels, along with Paul, that he is himself the worst of sinners. But then as he looks to the cross, he sees that Jesus was his atoning sacrifice. He sees that Jesus bore his sins in His own body, and that the wrath of God—the wrath which he, a sinner, should have borne—was expended completely and totally upon the holy Son of God. And in this view of Calvary, he sees the love of God.

The love of God has no meaning apart from Calvary. And Calvary has no meaning apart from the holy and just wrath of God. Jesus did not die just to give us peace and a purpose in life; He died to save us from the wrath of God. He died to reconcile us to a holy God who was alienated from us because of our sin. He died to ransom us from the penalty of sin—the punishment of everlasting destruction, shut out from the presence of the Lord. He died that we, the just objects of God's wrath, should become, by His grace, heirs of God and co-heirs with Him.

Do you have that assurance that your past, present, and future sins are forgiven by Christ Jesus because of what He did on the cross? If not, you can. In 1 John 1:9 we read, "If we confess our sins, he is faithful and just and will forgive us our sins and purify us from all unrighteousness."

Through God's Word you can be assured that your sins will not be on your permanent record as you stand before God on judgment day.

Thoughts for Action

❦ Confess any and all sins (past, present, future) and ask God to forgive them and to purify you from all your sins.

❦ Record this date in your journal.

❦ If you have a Bible, write today's date on the first inside page and write Romans 8:2 and 1 John 1:9 down as references.

❦ Tell a friend of your decision.

Additional Scripture Reading

Luke 18:9-14   Romans 5:14-21

Love Is Very Patient and Kind

Scripture Reading: 1 Corinthians 13:4-13

Key Verse: 1 Corinthians 13:4
> *Love is patient, love is kind. It does not envy, it does not boast, it is not proud.*

Our dear friends Bill and Carole Thornburgh know about showing love. In 1987 Bill was diagnosed with leukemia. Eighteen months and three rounds of chemotherapy treatment later, Bill went to be with our Lord. Soon afterward, Carole was reading a novel where the main character, who was dying of cancer, left a letter for her husband and another for her young children to read when they became adults. Carole desperately wished that Bill had left her a note.

Several days later, when she was getting ready to visit Bill's sister, Carole decided to take some of Bill's old books to her. While going through the books, Carole found an envelope addressed to her from Bill. He had written Carole an Easter card two years earlier, and she had tucked it away in a book. Upon rediscovering the card now, she was so thankful to God for her husband's written words. At Christmastime 1989, Carole had a precious Easter card from her beloved husband. It read:

A Tearful Week
A Long Week
A Hard Week
A Lonely Week
A Painful Week
A Revealing Week
A Recovering Week
A Reassuring Week
A Peace Week
A Rededication Week
A Friendship Week
A Love Week
A Roller Coaster Week
A Renewal Week
A Glorious Week
A Victorious Week
A Life Changing Week
But A Week I Will Never Lose Sight Of

May God be our source of true love and friendship. You have been so good these days. I love you for it. You have been all a husband would desire. Forgive me, Sweet, for not keeping our love fresh. I love you.

Happy Easter and Happy Beginnings,

Bill

Bill and Carole spoke openly of their love for one another, and Bill's words offered Carole a sense of his presence when he was gone.

. Learn the language of love. Each of us who is married needs to learn how to say, "I love you." And I'm not talking only about speaking aloud those three powerful words (although that's an important thing to do!). We need to also say, "I love you" through our sensitivity to our spouse, through our manners and our respect. Sometimes, for instance, as Bob

is leaving on errands, he will ask if there's anything he can get for me while he's out. Once in a while he might hear me say that I'd like a certain new book and—what do you know?—it shows up unexpectedly for no special reason. These are just some of the ways that Bob shows me that he loves me.

And I show Bob that I love him with an evening at the theater, a new shirt, or his favorite Southern fried chicken for dinner. However I choose to show my love, I say aloud to Bob, "Just another way to say, 'I love you!'" Little acts of kindness like this are powerful and effective ways to strengthen your friendship with your mate. Such little acts of thoughtfulness show that you do not take your loved one for granted.

Certain rituals and traditions in our family also enable us to express our love for one another. We kiss each other goodnight and say, "May God bless your sleep." We celebrate our love on anniversaries and birthdays by giving each other small gifts. We telephone one another when we're apart, visit one of two favorite restaurants on special occasions, go out to lunch, attend the theater, and share hugs and (my contribution) corny jokes. All of these things—spontaneous little acts as well as carefully planned events—make for a special friendship.

One word of caution! Be sure that you are expressing your love in the language—the words and the actions—that your spouse will understand! Just because you feel loved when he plans a special dinner out doesn't mean that he feels loved when you do the same! Be a student of your husband. Know what best communicates to him the love you have. And keep your eyes open for common, everyday events that give you the chance to express that love!

Bob and I continually strive to make sure that our love is patient, kind, that it does not envy, does not boast, or is not proud. It's a lifetime of challenges in developing a Christlike expression of love one to another.

Jerry and Barbara Cook offer another way to tell your husband—who is, I hope, your best friend—that you love him.

— ❦ —

I Need You

I need you in my times of strength and in my
weakness;
I need you when you hurt as much as when I hurt.
There is no longer the choice as to what we will
share.
We will either share all of life or be fractured per-
sons.
I didn't marry you out of need or to be needed.
We were not driven by instincts or emptiness;
We made a choice to love.
But I think something supernatural happens at the
point of marriage commitment (or maybe it's actu-
ally natural).
A husband comes into existence; a wife is born.
He is a whole man before and after, but at a point
in time he becomes a man who also is a husband;
That is—a man who needs his wife.
She is a whole woman before and after.
But from now on she needs him.
She is herself but now also part of a new unit.
Maybe this is what is meant in saying,
"What God hath joined together."
Could it be He really does something special at "I
do"?
Your despair is mine even if you don't tell me
about it.
But when you do tell, the sharing is easier for me;
And you also can then share from my strength in
that weakness.[18]

*Father God, I sincerely want this type of love for
myself and for all those whom I meet. Give me the
desire and strength to love others as You have loved
me. Protect me in this endeavor so that I will only*

love in an honorable way and express my love in a language that the person I care for will understand. Amen.

Thoughts for Action

❧ Do something for your husband that you hate doing: Iron his shirts, cook him breakfast, make his lunch, wash his car, cook his favorite meal, run an errand.

❧ Send him flowers at work.

❧ Let him warm his cold feet in bed.

❧ Spread rose petals all over the bedroom.

Additional Scripture Reading

1 Peter 4:7-11   1 John 4:7-21

☑ ☐ ☐

Your Husband's Friend

Scripture Reading: Genesis 2:18-23

Key Verse: Genesis 2:18
> The Lord God said, "It is not good for the man to be alone. I will make a helper, suitable for him."

Genesis 2:18-23 is a beautiful picture of how God created not only the first woman and wife, but also the first friend. A wife is indeed to be her husband's friend, and that has truly been my experience. Through the years, the love Bob and I have for each other has grown, and we have become each other's best friend. This passage from Genesis suggests that is exactly what God intends for a married couple. Let's look closely at this section of Scripture.

- God gives the woman to the man to be "a helper, suitable for him" (2:18). Do you consider yourself a helper or a hindrance to your husband? To his work? To his time at home? Are you "suitable" or unsuitable when it comes to recognizing and meeting his needs? Where could you be more helpful to him? If you're not sure, why not ask him?

- God creates woman from man's rib (2:21-22). Earlier in Genesis, we learn that God created human beings in His image (1:27). The fact that each of us is created in God's image calls us to honor and respect one another. Consider for a moment that your husband was made by God in His image, just as you were. How, then, should you treat him? Acknowledging that your husband has been created in the image of God calls you, I believe, to respect and honor him and to offer him love and friendship.

• Adam perceived Eve as part of his own bone and own flesh (2:23). If, like Adam, I rightly understand that Bob is actually part of me, I will want to treat him as well as I treat myself. I will want to take good care of him and provide for his every need. This kind of wife's love provides a good foundation for the kind of friendship a wife can give her man.

Consider the following definition of a friend.

And what is a friend? Many things...A friend is someone you are comfortable with, someone whose company you prefer. A friend is someone you can count on—not only for support, but for honesty.

A friend is one who believes in you...someone with whom you can share your dreams. In fact, a real friend is a person you want to share all of life with...and the sharing doubles the fun.

When you are hurting and you can share your struggle with a friend, it eases the pain. A friend offers you safety and trust...Whatever you say will never be used against you.

A friend will laugh with you, but not at you...A friend will pray with you...and for you.

My friend is one who hears my cry of pain,
who senses my struggle, who shares my lows as
well as my highs.[19]

In such a friendship, nothing is hidden. Such friendship is built on trust, and such friendship takes time to grow and develop. What better context for this kind of friendship to grow than your marriage? How does your marriage measure up against this description? If you and your husband don't yet share this kind of friendship, don't wait for him to reach out. Take the initial step and see how he responds. If you have tried before and not been well received, ask God to guide and bless your efforts and then risk reaching out again.

Father God, I want You to know that I want to be a friend to my husband. I want to fulfill the role for which I was made. Let my husband know that my desires for him come from my friendship with him and not from wanting to take away his freedom. Amen.

Thoughts for Action

❧ Do something with your husband that you don't normally like to do: maybe a ball game, a "man's" movie, the theater, fishing, hiking, or the beach.

❧ Write your mate a note expressing how much you enjoy him as a friend.

❧ Add a dimmer to your bedroom light switch.

Additional Scripture Reading

Proverbs 18:24   Amos 3:3
Ecclesiastes 4:9

How to Attract Your Mate

Scripture Reading: 1 Peter 3:3-5a

Key Verse: 1 Peter 3:3

> *Your beauty should not come from outward adornment, such as braided hair and the wearing of gold jewelry and fine clothes.*

What is attractive? Our Scripture today talks about God's perspective on beauty and attractiveness.

Scripture calls women to be godly and to develop an inward beauty, and that's of first importance. But wise women today also work to make themselves pleasing to their husband's eye—and that's right on target. When a wife looks good, a husband looks at her often and likes what he sees. A pleasing appearance will invite your husband to touch and hold you—and no one else. Your husband wants to be proud of you whether at home or in public. Besides, doesn't looking nice make you feel better about yourself?

My mother wore current fashions and popular colors even though we were a low middle-class family. (You don't have to have a lot of money to look attractive!) She always looked fashionable. She never left home with curlers in her hair or a bandanna wrapped around her head—she didn't want to embarrass herself if she ran into friends.

Every married woman needs to ask herself, "Am I looking my best when I am with my husband? Is he proud of my personal appearance?" If you feel you could make yourself more appealing and attractive, there are many resources available, including books and magazines, friends who will give suggestions, color and wardrobe seminars, and department store consultants who can assist you in developing a new you. Or you might follow the example of a friend of mine...

Jan has a specific plan of action to get ready for her husband's arrival home. Each day at 4:00 P.M. , she takes a shower or bath, powders and perfumes, combs her hair, and dresses informally. She lives according to the Barnes motto: "A husband should be sad when he leaves for work in the morning, and a wife should be glad to see him come home in the evening." When Jan's husband arrives, her appearance shows that she has been waiting for him and that she cares that he has returned. I encourage you to pay attention to how you look for your husband. You—and he and your marriage—will definitely benefit!

As you strive to look and feel your best, always remember today's key verse. It provides balance when it comes to dress and style. As Christian women we have to be sensitive not to be conformed to the world's standard of beauty, but to look at the inner qualities that develop us into godly women.

> *Father God, show me how I can be appealing to my husband both inside and out. Guide my efforts at inner beauty and outer attractiveness. Truly let my husband be sad when he leaves home for work, and give me a joy and happiness when he comes home each evening. Amen.*

Thoughts for Action

❧ In your journal list several areas where you feel you could be more attractive.

❦ Alongside each entry write what action you will do to get it accomplished.

❦ Try a new way to say, "I love you!" to your husband. Write him a love letter, a poem, or a song. Hiding places for love notes and small gifts: under the pillow, in the glove compartment of his car, in the medicine cabinet near his razor, in his briefcase, under his dinner plate, etc.

❦ Why be romantic? Why bother? Simple. It will improve your quality of life.

Additional Scripture Reading

1 Timothy 2:9-10   Song of Songs 1:1-17

☑ ☐ ☐

Your Most Important Decision

Scripture Reading: Joshua 24:14-15

Key Verse: Joshua 24:15

> But as for me and my household, we will serve the Lord.

Some decisions we make in life are everlasting. We see throughout history how proper and improper decisions have changed the history of mankind.

Joshua faced the same dilemma for his family as we do for our family. Which God to worship? The gods of the world or *the* God—Jehovah?

Choosing whom to worship is the most basic question of our life. Joshua was a man of courage, strength, determination, and faith. He was a leader to his family and nation. As recorded in today's Scripture reading, Joshua states that we worship the gods we want to. For Joshua and his family, they will serve the Lord.

Which of the gods will you serve? Your life today is a consequence of the decisions you made yesterday. Are you tired of being a slave to poor decisions of the past? If so, you can have the freedom and joy of being in Christ. You do not have to continue to suffer the pain of yesterday; today you can commit to turning your life around.

Paul writes in Romans 10:9-10, "That if you confess with your mouth, 'Jesus is Lord,' and believe in your heart that God raised him from the dead, you will be saved. For it is with your heart that you believe and are justified, and it is with your mouth that you confess and are saved."

Can you make a decision today about this promise? It will be the best decision of your life. Don't delay. Don't wait until it's too late. The writer of Ecclesiastes 3:1 states, "There is a time for everything, and a season for every activity under heaven."

Three times a soldier in a hospital picked up the hymn "Will You Go?" which was scattered as a tract. Twice he threw it down. The last time, he read it, thought about it, and, taking his pencil, wrote deliberately in the margin these words: "By the grace of God, I will try to go, John Waugh, Company G, Tenth Regiment, P.R.V.C." That night, he went to a prayer meeting, read his resolution, requested prayers for his salvation, and said, "I am not ashamed of Christ now; but I am ashamed of myself for having been so long ashamed of Him." He was killed a few months later. How timely was his resolution!

Today is the appointed time. Make that decision for the first time, or reconfirm a previous decision that you and your family will serve the Lord.

Father God, each day I must choose what god I will worship. May I, as Joshua did, choose Jehovah God. I want to serve You with all my heart and soul. Please renew that desire in me on a daily basis. I love You. Amen.

Thoughts for Action

❦ Make the decision to serve the Lord today.

❦ Record this date in your journal.

❦ If you have a Bible, write today's date on the first inside page and write Romans 8:1 and 1 John 1:9 down as a reference.

❦ Tell a friend of your decision.

Additional Scripture Reading

Romans 3:23	Acts 16:30-31
Romans 6:23	Ephesians 2:8-9

Worthy of Love

Scripture Reading: Matthew 22:36-40

Key Verse: Matthew 22:37-39

> *"Love the Lord your God with all your heart and with all your soul and with all your mind." This is the first and greatest commandment. And the second is like it: "Love your neighbor as yourself."*

Jesus' words in today's key verse are from Deuteronomy 6:4-9. The Jewish nation used these words as part of their Shema, which became Judaism's basic confession of faith. According to rabbinic law, this passage was to be recited every morning and night. This passage stresses the uniqueness of God, precludes the worship of other gods, and demands a total love commitment.

In Matthew 22 Jesus was asked, "Teacher, which is the greatest commandment in the Law?" Jesus gave two commandments which stress three loves: the love of God, the love of your neighbor, and the love of self. We know we ought to love God and to be kind and love our neighbors, but somehow we have a difficult time knowing how to love ourselves. I have met many women who do not understand this concept. As women, we always seem to be giving so much to others in our family that there is no time left for us.

As a young woman and a new bride, then as a new mother, I was always tired. I had no energy left over for me and we most certainly didn't have any money left over from our budget to give me anything. So what did I do for myself? Not very much. After studying this passage of Scripture, I was challenged to study the subject of personal worth. I was careful not to put an overemphasis on self, but to take a balanced and moderate approach that would let me grow as an individual. I knew if God was going to make me a complete and functioning person in the body of Christ, I had to develop a wholesome approach to this area of caring for myself.

As I began to look about me, I discovered women who had a mistrust of themselves and who had begun to withhold love and self-acceptance, women who had no idea that God had a plan for their life, women whose lives reflected fear, guilt, and mistrust of other people. These women did not understand that God had given them certain divine dignity which could make it possible for them to love themselves, and realize they are worthy of love. I also noticed that women would relate to their friends, their husbands, and their children either positively or negatively depending how well they understood this principle.

I can remember one Friday morning in a home Bible study. We were studying a marriage book, and Amy spoke up and said that she didn't take care of her personal self because her father had told her at a young age that pretty girls with good clothes and nice figures stood a better chance of being molested by older boys and men as they grew up. At that time Amy decided she would not let herself be molested by an older man, so she began to gain weight and wear sloppy clothes. She even remarked that her husband liked her this way because other men didn't try to flirt with her. He felt safe from any competition.

Over the next several months in our weekly study, I began to share with Amy how this fear was put there by Satan and not by God. I took extra time encouraging her to be all that God had for her. We looked at her eating habits and why she chose certain foods. After a while she began to seek professional counseling to understand what she was hiding behind. If you could see Amy today, you would see a fine young woman who has a totally new image and who shares with other women in full confidence. Because of Amy's appropriate self-appraisal, her husband has also joined a support group at church and has lessened his fears from his own insecurities.

What is anger? What is hatred? It is really fear. And what is fear? It is a feeling of being threatened, a deep feeling of insecurity. And what causes that feeling of insecurity? It is a lack of confidence in our ability to cope with threatening situations. And lack of self-confidence is the result of too low a value of yourself. You aren't able to love yourself because of what you think you are!

R.C. Sproul says that "lack of faith" is a "lack of trust" that God is capable of doing what He has promised He will do.

It takes a lot of faith to love. People who cannot love themselves do not dare to love. They are afraid they'll be spurned or rejected. Why do they have that fear? Because they do not trust themselves or rate themselves high enough to believe they'll be loved. And why do they fear rejection? Because rejection will only put salt in the wounds, proving again that they aren't worthy.

In Genesis 1:26-27 it says, "Then God said, 'Let us make man in our image, in our likeness...' So God created man in his own image, in the image of God he created him; male and female he created them." In verse 31 the Scripture says, "God saw all that he had made, and it was very good." We were spiritually designed to enjoy the honor that befits a prince of heaven. There is a basic need to recognize the dignity of the human being to be a child of God.

George Gallup, Jr., of the Gallup organization, conducted a poll on the self-esteem of the American public. The poll conclusively demonstrated that people with a positive self-image demonstrate the following qualities:

1. They have a high moral and ethical sensitivity.

2. They have a strong sense of family.

3. They are far more successful in interpersonal relationships.

4. Their perspective of success is viewed in terms of interpersonal relationships, not in crass materialistic terms.

5. They're far more productive on the job.

6. They are far lower in incidents of chemical addictions. (Current research shows that 80 percent of all suicides are related to alcohol and drug addiction.)

7. They are more likely to get involved in social and political activities in their community.

8. They are far more generous to charitable institutions and give far more generously to relief causes.[20]

As contributing members of our family, church, community, and society, each of us wants these positive qualities.

It seems the majority of our churches struggle in implementing the three loves of Deuteronomy and Matthew. But people who view God as a personal, loving, and forgiving Being, and relate to Him in such a personal way, do develop a strong, healthy sense of self-worth. Make sure you are in a church that teaches these aspects of the gospel.

Paul teaches in Philippians 4:13 that, "I can do everything through him who gives me strength." Using this principle, we can realize that Christ gives us the inner strength to care for ourselves. We must choose to love ourselves. There are many who say that self-love is evil and wrong, but I don't believe that's true. I want to encourage you to take time for yourself each day. Time for yourself gives you time to renew your mind, body, and spirit. Not only will you be rewarded, but so will those who come in contact with you daily.

Father God, I don't want to become self-centered,
but I do want to understand the value You have given

me because You gave Your Son. Please reveal to me
those areas of my life that I find difficult to love.
Help me to base my sense of self-worth on You.
Amen.

Thoughts for Action

🍎 In your journal write down five things you like about yourself.

🍎 Also, write down five things you want to improve about
yourself.

🍎 After each item on the second list write one or two things
you are going to do to improve that area of your life.

🍎 Take a stroll at the beach, in the woods, through the snow,
on a windy trail. Ponder how wonderfully you are made
(Psalm 139).

Additional Scripture Reading

Deuteronomy 6:4-9   Philippians 4:13

Martha and Mary and Me

Scripture Reading: Luke 10:38-42

Key Verse: Luke 10:41-42

> *"Martha, Martha," the Lord answered, "you are worried and upset about many things, but only one thing is needed. Mary has chosen what is better, and it will not be taken away from her."*

———— ❦ ————

Confession of a Clutter Bug

Lord, bless this mess—
All of it's mine.
It keeps me in distress
All of the time.
Each item I save,
And think I may need,
Is an outward sign
Of inner greed.
Help me to let go and
Quit keeping everything.
I'm a clutter bug I know,
But You are the King of Kings!
By Your power I ask

195

For freedom—yes release.
Help me in my task
To let go of things, please?

—Tina Posey
Alabama

I have a confession to make: I've been more like Martha than like Mary. I desire to be like Mary, but my Martha side keeps getting in the way.

With a basic knowledge of people differences, we can see that Martha is the doer. Author and speaker Florence Littauer would identify her as a Powerful Choleric ("Let's do it my way"). Martha has a desire to control the situation. She has the ability to take charge of anything instantly. She is valuable in work because she can accomplish more than anyone else in a shorter time, and she's usually right. But she has weaknesses too. She's often bossy, domineering, autocratic, insensitive, and impatient. She is usually unwilling to delegate or to give credit to others.

On the other hand, Mary would be identified as Peaceful Phlegmatic ("Let's do it the easy way"). Mary wants to avoid conflict and to keep peace. She has a balance in life, an even disposition, and usually a dry sense of humor. Her personality is pleasing. She is valuable in work because she cooperates and is a calming influence. She keeps peace, mediates between contentious people, and objectively solves problems. However, she will often lack decisiveness, enthusiasm, and energy.

Many of my readers express this frustration of the struggle between Martha and Mary. They can relate to the following:

My Martha Side

My house is a tyrant, demanding each hour. Imperiously ordering: "Sweep, mop and scour! Do the dishes, the laundry, then iron, dust and cook! And there's mending to do if you'll just take a look. Now, Martha, get busy and don't waste a minute; dirt is a sin, and you're wallowing in it!"

My Mary Side

My housework can wait...there's a friend I must see, who's lonely and frightened, she's looking for me. Then I'll tidy up quickly and hurry to hear that fine missionary we support every year. Home again, "Father, thank You, please help me to care for the hungry and homeless who live in despair."

Mary-Martha-Me

Martha nags me to keep my house spotless each day; and Mary says gently, "I need time to pray." Martha's concerned with "what neighbors might think if they dropped in and found dishes stacked in the sink." While Mary chides, "Selfish! I think it's a crime if you don't share with others your talents and time."

My Prayer

Oh God, in compassion, so order my days that Mary might serve Thee and Martha may praise Thee.

Father God, I desire a balanced life. Reveal to me how I can be a Martha and a Mary. They were both virtuous in the way they ministered to You, and I have only pure desires to serve You as well. Please show me the way. Amen.

Thoughts for Action

❦ Write down in your journal the struggles you have with being a Martha.

❦ Write down in your journal the struggles you have with being a Mary.

❦ In each case state what you might do to come to a middle ground. Pray to God that He will give you the desires of your heart to serve God and family in a more balanced lifestyle!

Additional Scripture Reading

Luke 9:57-62   Matthew 4:4

Continually Seek God's Wisdom

Scripture Reading: Proverbs 1:1-7

Key Verse: Proverbs 1:7
The fear of the Lord is the beginning of knowledge,
but fools despise wisdom and discipline.

If you go to God looking for knowledge and wisdom, you'll find it—and the wisdom that comes from God is the kind that will protect you. God is the giver of all good things. It just makes sense to listen as he speaks!

A lot of people have the idea that following God is a big burden. But that's not the way it works in real life. Actually, when you open your heart to receive wisdom from God, you'll find that it's a pleasing thing. It actually feels good to be guided by God and follow his paths.

...The more you experience doing what is right, the clearer your decisions of right and wrong will become. It starts out with the glimmer of the faint light of daybreak— you get a little sense of what is right and you act on it. As you continue to make right decisions (using the words of Scripture and dependable counselors to help you), everything becomes a lot clearer and brighter and less confusing. What once seemed murky and hard to distinguish takes on the intensity of the noonday sun. So don't worry if you sometimes seem to be walking along dimly lit paths. Keep on doing what you know to be right, and everything will get a lot clearer. There's no reason to stumble when wisdom provides the light.

...Sometimes it seems as if the world rewards the wrong people! Public immorality, official corruption, random violence, and just plain bad manners almost seem the standard of success, and the sleaziest, most indecent people seem to be making money, gaining fame, and being elected to office.

But don't be fooled. In the end, your attempt to...live out the life that God has designed will be rewarded. By your very life, you'll add to the joy in your family, neighborhood, city, state, and nation—not to mention the joy that fills the heavens.[21]

Solomon's wise sayings offer us advice on how to conduct ourselves in various situations in everyday life. His fundamental instruction is to fear and trust the Lord. Solomon challenges us to continually seek God's wisdom in the decisions we must make each day.

This type of knowledge goes beyond academic accomplishments to moral responsibility. It focuses in on decision-making and shows itself best in the disciplining of our character. We raise our children to be lawyers, doctors, teachers, sales people, musicians, but do we ever purposefully raise our children to be good? We need a country where parents want to raise children to be good. Our country and world are desperately in need of good people.

We must begin to think clearly and scripturally if we are to survive the present cultural war in America. In regard to right and wrong, we must arrive at consistent answers that go along with our theological understanding of Scripture. We can't be swayed by what the secular world says. We must go to Scripture to see what God instructs us to do (see Romans 12:1-2). We must continually seek God's wisdom.

——— ❦ ———

Father God, I want to be a woman who seeks after Your knowledge. Show me Your ways that I might acknowledge You as God. Help me to see that You are all that I will ever need. Amen.

Thoughts for Action

❦ List in your journal five decisions that need to be answered today. On what basis will they be answered? Scriptural or secular?

❦ Get in the habit of answering basic questions from a theological framework.

❦ Select a verse of Scripture that will be your theme verse for life. I use Matthew 6:33.

Additional Scripture Reading

Romans 12:1-2   James 3:13-18
Proverbs 3:1-18

□ □ □

Memories of
the Garden Bench

Scripture Reading: Philippians 1:3-11

Key Verse: Philippians 1:3
I thank my God every time I remember you.

It was a warm sunny day for January in Riverside, California. Two of our five grandchildren were helping us enjoy this fine day. Ten-and-a-half-year-old Christine was helping her Grammy Em plan and cook the dinner. She was picking flowers to arrange for our dinner table. PaPa Bob and Bevan were raking the garden, and picking oranges, avocados, and lemons off our trees that surround our property.

As the afternoon progressed, our working men became warm and tired.

Christine said, "Grammy, let's have tea." That's all it takes for me to stop whatever I'm doing and put the kettle on for Christine and me to have tea. In the process, we poured the men a tall glass of fresh juice on ice and prepared some yummy-for-the-tummy snacks. We carried the treats up the hill to PaPa and Bevan. How happy they were to receive the refreshment. They thanked us and headed for the bench that sits under a large shady avocado tree overlooking the grounds and our quaint, tree-lined little Rumsey Drive which winds by our barn.

As Christine and I left them, we headed back toward the house. Christine took my hand and said, "Grammy, I love you." "I love you, too, Christine," I said.

I prepared the tea kettle, and Christine pulled down the tea pot and put the teacups on the table with our special silver tea spoons. We toasted thick sourdough bread that we spread with jam and butter. It was an instant tea party—just Christine and me.

That night as my Bob and I crawled in bed, we began to share about our day with the oh-so-wonderful grandchildren.

"What do a PaPa and seven-year-old grandson talk about on the bench under the big avocado tree?" I asked.

"Oh, very special things," Bob replied. "Boys talk just like you girls talk."

I could still picture PaPa Bob and seven-year-old Bevan— with smudges of dirt on both their faces—sitting on that bench.

Bob continued, "I told Bevan, 'Someday, Bevan, when PaPa's in heaven and you drive down Rumsey Drive as a man, you'll look at this bench we are sitting on and you can remember the day that Grammy Em and sister Christine served us jam and toast with a glass of juice.' Then Bevan said, 'Not only will I remember, but I will bring my son and someday he will bring his son and point to the bench and tell him about the toast and jam we ate on the bench under that big avocado tree over there.'"

How does a little boy understand and think through the process of generations?

How blessed we are to have the God-given opportunity to teach our children and grandchildren about the beauty of God's creations, life and death, and most of all about God the Father, God, the Son, and God, the Holy Spirit.

Father God, we think we only live for today but
Scripture tells us to look to the future and eternity.
The world wants us to conform to the pressures of

the here and now and focus on the temporal. Help me to take time to develop a future orientation for myself and my family. What You have done for us in the past gives us hope for the future. Amen.

Thoughts for Action

- Take a child's hand. Take a walk and talk to each other.

- Give a cup of refreshment to someone today—a cup of tea or a glass of juice.

- Tell someone, "I love you."

Additional Scripture Reading

1 Corinthians 1:4   Deuteronomy 6:7
Psalm 67:1

Keeping a Tight Rein

Scripture Reading: James 1:19-27

Key Verse: James 1:26

> *If anyone considers himself religious and yet does not keep a tight rein on his tongue, he deceives himself and his religion is worthless.*

In *All I Really Need to Know I Learned in Kindergarten,* Robert Fulghum suggests that serenity and a quiet spirit is very much needed in our noisy world. He tells of villagers in the Solomon Islands who felled a tree by screaming at it for 30 days. The tree died, confirming the Islanders' theory that hollering kills a living thing's spirit. Fulghum then considers the things that he and his neighbors yell at: the wife, the kids, the telephone, the lawnmower that won't start, traffic, umpires, machines. Then he offers this observation:

> Don't know what good it does. Machines and things just sit there. Even kicking doesn't always help. As for people, well, the Solomon Islanders may have a point. Yelling at living things does tend to kill the spirit in them. Sticks and stones may break our bones, but words will break our hearts.[22]

Oh, if we could only remember this each time we want to overpower someone with a loud voice. How much better a quiet and gentle spirit! How much better tranquillity and serenity!

One of the ways we try to get control over a person or situation is by raising our voices. However, that is just the opposite of what we need to do. Try lowering your voice next time you're tempted to raise it. The world already has people who are dead in spirit because someone didn't realize that loud voices can kill. You can have a tremendous positive effect upon those who are near you. Let others remember you as a loving person, not a screamer.

Thoughts for Action

❦ Plant a tree today; water it and give it some vitamin B-1. It's a positive experience to see things grow.

❦ In your journal evaluate how you use your words and your voice in your life. If you aren't satisfied with your behavior, list several areas where you want to change. At the same time, list what actions you are going to do to make changes.

❦ Today practice lowering your voice when you feel like raising it.

❦ Apologize to someone—in person, by phone, or in a letter—to whom you have talked too harshly.

Additional Scripture Reading

Ephesians 4:29   Psalm 34:12-13

A Wife of Noble Character

Scripture Reading: Proverbs 12:1-7

Key Verse: Proverbs 12:4
A wife of noble character is her husband's crown, but a disgraceful wife is like decay in his bones.

Major Sullivan Ballou wrote this letter to his devoted wife, Sarah, a week before the first battle of Bull Run, near Manassas, Virginia. Sarah must have been a wife of noble character that truly was a crown to her soldier husband.

July 14, 1861
Camp Clerk, Washington, D.C.

My very dear Sarah,
The indications are very strong that we shall move in a few days—perhaps tomorrow. Lest I should not be able to write again, I feel impelled to write a few lines that may fall under your eye when I shall be no more...

I have no misgivings about, or lack of confidence in, the cause in which I am engaged, and my courage does not halt or falter. I know how strongly American Civilization now leans on the triumph of the Government, and how great a debt we owe to those who went before us through the blood and sufferings of the Revolution. And I am willing—perfectly willing—to lay down all my joys in this life, to help maintain this Government, and to pay that debt.

Sarah, my love for you is deathless; it seems to bind me with mighty cables that nothing but Omnipotence could break; and yet my love of Country comes over me like a strong wind and bears me unresistibly on with all these chains to the battlefield.

The memories of the blissful moments I have spent with you come creeping over me, and I feel most gratified to God and to you that I have enjoyed them so long. And hard it is for me to give them up and burn to ashes the hopes of future years, when, God willing we might still have lived and loved together, and seen our sons grow up to honorable manhood, around us. I have, I know, but few and small claims upon Divine Providence, but something whispers to me-perhaps it is the wafted prayer of my little Edgar, that I shall return to my loved ones unharmed. If I do not, my dear Sarah, never forget how much I love you, and when my last breath escapes me on the battlefield, it will whisper your name. Forgive my many faults, and the many pains I have caused you. How thoughtless and foolish I have often times been! How gladly would I wash out with my tears every little spot upon your happiness...

But, O Sarah! if the dead can come back to this earth and flit unseen around those they loved, I shall always be near you; in the gladdest days and in the darkest nights... *always, always,* and if there be a soft breeze upon your cheek, it shall be my breath, as the cool air fans your throbbing temple, it shall be my spirit passing by. Sarah, do not mourn me dead; think I am gone and wait for thee, for we shall meet again.[23]

Sullivan Ballou was killed at the first battle of Bull Run, leaving his wife these few, beautiful lines of love. She undoubtedly thought of her beloved husband whenever a soft breeze touched her cheek. Her husband had been both strong and sensitive, both tough and tender. As his letter reflects, he faced death with courage, standing strong in his convictions and unwavering in his commitment to his country, his wife, and his God. And I would guess that some of his courage resulted from a wife who believed in him, encouraged him, and made him her hero.

Supporting your man will indeed encourage him to be the man—and husband and father—that God wants him to be. Like Sullivan Ballou, who was both tough and tender, your husband can come to know the strength of his masculinity. He can know the balance between strong and sensitive that God intended when He made man. I'm sure God looked down upon Major Ballou and said, "It was good." You can help your man earn those same words of praise, and he will praise you at the gates.

May we all strive to be a wife of noble character and our husband's crown.

> *Father God, I desire to be a woman of character. I want to find pleasure in Your sight, and I want to be a crown unto my husband. Please bring into my life those women who will show me how to develop Christian character. May my husband be receptive to my changes. I so want him to know that I love him very much. I never want to be a disgrace to him. Amen.*

Thoughts for Action

❦ Do you consider yourself to be a woman of noble character?

🐞 What makes you answer yes?

🐞 What makes you answer no?

🐞 What changes need to be made in your life to become a wife of noble character?

🐞 List a few activities that you will undertake to make these changes.

🐞 Meditate on these:

—Find good men and women to emulate.

—Carry no grudges. They'll weigh you down.

—Every day look for some little thing you can do to improve how you do your job.

Additional Scripture Reading

Philippians 4:8   Romans 14:17-19

Don't Be Afraid

Scripture Reading: Mark 16:1-8

Key Verse: Mark 16:6a
Don't be afraid.

Steven R. Covey, in his book *The Seven Habits of Highly Effective People,* tells a story that reflects the need for renewal and reawakening in our lives.

You are walking in the woods and encounter a man sawing down a tree. He looks exhausted, and he tells you he's been working nearly half the day. But when you suggest that he take a short break and sharpen his saw so his work will go more quickly, he refuses. "I'm too busy sawing," he declares. [24]

If we are to stay on top of the pile rather than under the pile, we must take time to sharpen the saws of our lives. As I speak in front of various groups, I find many women who are defeated and burned out from their roles in life. Many women express to me, "If I only had time for myself, I would stop and smell the roses!"

Below I have given you several ideas that will help you care for yourself. When we renew our lives, we are better equipped to handle stress and fear. If you are afraid, uptight, tense, or short-tempered, maybe you need a touch of renewal for yourself.

In the "Thoughts for Action" section, you will find several activities that will give you a fresh approach to life.

Reach out, risk, and try several of them.

Thoughts for Action

Physical

🥀 Get a professional massage, sauna, and steam bath.

🥀 Have your hair and nails done. Get a pedicure.

🥀 Exercise regularly by walking, jogging, doing aerobics, etc.

🥀 Read a book on nutrition and begin to change your eating habits.

🥀 Take a stress-management class.

🥀 Take a quiet bubble bath by candlelight.

🥀 Take a stroll on the beach, by the lake, or along a mountain trail.

🥀 Plant a flower and/or vegetable garden.

🥀 Walk or run in the rain.

Mental

🥀 Listen to good music.

🥀 Read a good magazine or book.

🥀 Retreat to a spot for a quiet time of meditating and reflecting.

🥀 Spend time alone.

🥀 Write a poem.

🥀 Write a letter to an old friend.

🥀 Plan your next three months' goals.

🥀 Enroll in a class at your local college.

❦ Think of possible changes in your life.

❦ List everything for which you are thankful.

❦ Memorize a poem.

❦ Learn to play an instrument.

❦ Go to the beach and listen to the waves.

❦ Reach back to joyful times as a child and think about them.

Social/Emotional

❦ Have a good cry.

❦ Have breakfast or lunch with a friend.

❦ Go to the mall and people-watch.

❦ Have a friend over for tea or coffee (decaffeinated preferably).

❦ Spend a day doing anything you want.

❦ Spend a weekend with your husband in a quiet setting just to regroup.

❦ Visit a friend.

❦ Develop friendships with new people.

❦ Buy a bouquet of flowers for yourself.

❦ Donate time to a school, hospital, or church.

❦ Volunteer to collect money for United Way, the Cancer Society, or the Heart Association.

❦ Serve a friend in need.

Spiritual

❦ Read the Psalms.

❦ Meditate on Scripture.

❦ Read a spiritual book that you have had lying on your kitchen table for some time.

❦ Write your worries in the sand at the beach.

❦ Join a women's Bible study.

❦ Visit someone at the hospital or nursing home.

❦ Give of yourself.

❦ Examine your motives. Are they self-serving or serving others?

❦ Listen to good Christian music.

Make up your own lists of ideas under each of the headings. Learn to care for yourself. God felt it was such a valuable concept that He stated it as part of one of the two great commandments in Matthew 22:37-38. Jesus says, "Love the Lord your God with all your heart and with all your soul and with all your mind....Love your neighbor as yourself." The world needs to witness us Christians living these two great commandments. Begin today to walk your talk. Jesus went on to say that on these two commandments depend the whole law and prophets.

Yes, it's okay to care for yourself because Jesus said it was. Let's plan time in each of our days to care for ourselves.

Additional Scripture Reading
Isaiah 41:10,13   Exodus 20:2-18

Dwelling in the Sanctuary

Scripture Reading: Psalm 15:1-5

Key Verse: Psalm 15:1-5

> Lord, who may dwell in your sanctuary? Who may
> live on your holy hill? He whose walk is blameless
> and who does what is righteous, who speaks the truth
> from his heart and has no slander on his tongue, who
> does his neighbor no wrong and casts no slur on his
> fellowman, who despises a vile man but honors those
> who fear the Lord, who keeps his oath even when it
> hurts, who lends his money without usury and does
> not accept a bribe against the innocent. He who does
> these things will never be shaken.

In today's passage David describes the character of the person who qualifies to be a guest of God's sanctuary. The two parallel questions of verse 1 are answered in the following four verses by an eleven-fold description of the righteous person who is upright in deed, word and attitude, and finances. These qualities, which aren't natural, are imparted by God and by his Holy Spirit.

Let's see what we can learn from this great psalm about the person who may dwell in the Lord's sanctuary:

1. He walks blameless.
2. He does what is righteous.
3. He speaks the truth from his heart.
4. He has no slander on his tongue.
5. He does his neighbor no harm.
6. He casts no slur on his fellowman.
7. He despises a vile (evil) man.
8. He honors those who fear the Lord.
9. He keeps his oath even when it hurts.
10. He lends his money without usury.
11. He does not accept a bribe against the innocent.

These are honorable characteristics! We certainly can appreciate the virtue of this type of person. However, many times we look upon the life of a righteous person and say to ourselves, "It must be easy for her to be a Christian. She evidently doesn't have the struggles with sin like I do!" Yet anyone who is trying to live a righteous life knows that we must choose each day to serve the Lord. It isn't any easier for any of us. We must decide moment by moment to do what is right.

David closes this psalm by stating, "He who does these things will never be shaken." What a great promise. Now let's live it with great faith.

> *Father God, the Scripture tells me to dwell on those things which are honorable and pure in deed. I willfully decide today to believe and live the Scriptures as the saints of old, beginning with precept unto precept and line upon line. I want to be your woman. Amen.*

Thoughts for Action

❦ Think on these things:

1. Compliment someone today.

2. Begin reading a good book.

3. Find five things every day to thank God for.

4. Lose no opportunity to develop relationships with wise men and women whose outlook will rub off on you.

🍂 Choose one of the 11 points in today's study and concentrate on improving this area of your life.

Additional Scripture Reading

Psalm 27:5   Psalm 24:3-4
Joshua 24:14-15   Philippians 4:8

□ □ □

Earthquake

Scripture Reading: Matthew 24:6-13

Key Verse: Matthew 24:7b

> There will be famines and earthquakes in various places.

On January 17, 1994, at 4:31 A.M. in Southern California, the Los Angeles area was rocked by a magnitude 6.6 earthquake. Living one hour east of the epicenter, we felt the quake quite well. This quake shook up and down, not the rolling motions we've felt in the past. Almost all of Southern California awoke out of a dead sleep. Many ran into the streets or crawled under beds, desks, tables, and doorways. Our phone rang. It was our son Brad, "Dad, this was a bad one. Los Angeles has been hit hard." He was correct. Fatalities mounted and damages rose to billions of dollars. Freeways fell, fires broke out, and much, much more.

Only three months earlier Southern California had been hit by major fires, then rain caused mud slides in multi-million-dollar home areas. We have experienced most of what the Scripture talks about from riots, quakes, fire, and flooding. The safety factor in this part of the country has dropped dramatically, with drive-by shootings, gangs, carjackings, murders, and thefts of all kinds.

Yet, why are we surprised? Our text tells us that before the Lord returns these things will happen. We must be ready. Residents here keep bottled water, earthquake kits, gas shut-off valves, etc.—trying to prepare for the big hit. Well, January 17, 1994 was almost it. The cleanup and rebuilding took years. Yet time will pass, people will forget, and we'll proceed on with the fast pace of L.A. life.

More importantly, though, we must be ready in an eternal way. We need to prepare ourselves, spiritually and eternally, for the future quake of Jesus' return. He is coming again—just as the earth trembles at times. We don't know time, day, or place. Our Lord will come when we least expect Him.

I'll tell you from experience that when the earth quakes the fear flies through your body. But it will not be near the heated fear and trembling of those who are not ready upon the Lord's return. Jesus says in John 11:25-26 "I am the resurrection and the life. He who believes in me will live, even though he dies, and whoever lives and believes in me will never die." This is what we must believe to be ready. So simple, yet so many reject.

Remember, when comes the last call, we'll know that the Bible was true after all.

Believing is receiving.

> *Father God, I pray for those who do not believe in You as Savior of the world. May Your Spirit touch those hearts and open them to Your words. May we, as believers, be ready, taking the preparation time to pray for those who we know in our jobs, communities, and yes, even churches. Amen.*

Thoughts for Action

❦ Read 1 John today.

❦ Write in your journal the time you invited the Lord to be your Savior.

❦ Read this devotion to someone today.

Additional Scripture Reading

    Isaiah 29:5-7   Acts 16:26
    John 3:16

Believe What God Believes About You

Scripture Reading: 1 Corinthians 13:4-13

Key Verse: 1 Corinthians 13:4-13

> Love is patient, love is kind. It does not envy, it does not boast, it is not proud. It is not rude, it is not self-seeking, it is not easily angered, it keeps no record of wrongs. Love does not delight in evil but rejoices with the truth. It always protects, always trusts, always hopes, always perseveres.
>
> Love never fails. But where there are prophecies, they will cease; where there are tongues, they will be stilled; where there is knowledge, it will pass away. For we know in part and we prophesy in part, but when perfection comes, the imperfect disappears. When I was a child, I talked like a child, I thought like a child, I reasoned like a child. When I became a man, I put childish ways behind me. Now we see but a poor reflection as in a mirror; then we shall see face to face. Now I know in part; then I shall know fully, even as I am fully known.
>
> And now these three remain: faith, hope and love. But the greatest of these is love.

It's important to believe that we have value and that we are worthy to give of ourselves. This begins by knowing and accepting what our heavenly Father believes about us. Christian psychologist Dr. Dick Dickerson has written a paraphrase of 1 Corinthians 13 which beautifully summarizes how God looks at us. Read this aloud to yourself each morning and evening for the next 30 days, then evaluate how your feelings about yourself have changed:

Because God loves me, He is slow to lose patience with me.

Because God loves me, He takes the circumstances of my life and uses them in a constructive way for my growth.

Because God loves me, He does not treat me as an object to be possessed and manipulated.

Because God loves me, He has no need to impress me with how great and powerful He is because He is God. Nor does He belittle me as His child in order to show me how important He is.

Because God loves me, He is for me. He wants me to mature and develop in His love.

Because God loves me, He does not send down His wrath on every little mistake I make, of which there are many.

Because God loves me, He does not keep score of all my sins and then beat me over the head with them whenever He gets a chance.

Because God loves me, He is deeply grieved when I do not walk in the ways that please Him because He sees this as evidence that I don't trust Him and love Him as I should.

Because God loves me, He rejoices when I experience His power and strength and stand up under the pressure of life for His name's sake.

Because God loves me, He keeps working patiently with me even when I feel like giving up and can't see why He doesn't give up with me too.

Because God loves me, He keeps on trusting me when at times I don't even trust myself.

Because God loves me, He never says there is no hope for me, rather, He patiently works with me, loves me, and disciplines me in such a way that it is hard for me to understand the depth of His concern for me.

Because God loves me, He never forsakes me even though many of my friends might.[25]

"Please be patient with me. God isn't finished with me yet." That is certainly true! As we look at a particular area in our lives, we can be tempted to break into tears of discouragement because we feel so defeated. But God is still working in our lives, and He will never give up on us.

There is a void in each of our lives that cannot be filled by the world. We may leave God or put Him on hold, but He is always there. He patiently waits for us to run our race, becoming fatigued in the process, and then to turn back to Him.

As you become secure in God's love, you will discover that you need not surrender your caring for yourself to the opinions and judgments of others. *God is for you!*

> *Father God, negative inner voices would love to convince me that I am a nobody, but the Holy Spirit continually challenges me to believe that I am of value to God and will be with Jesus in Paradise. Can I believe God when He tells me that I was so important to Him that He gave His only Son, Jesus Christ, to die on the cross for my sins? Yes, I can! I am special to God. Let me believe it and live it. Amen.*

Thoughts for Action

- Buy 100 "Love" postage stamps.
- Buy a new recording of your favorite musical artist.

❦ Buy yourself a new novel by your favorite writer.

❦ Write in your journal, "God loves me and so do I" 25 times. Read it through twice. Believe what you write and read.

Additional Scripture Reading

1 John 4:10   Song of Songs 8:6-7
1 John 4:12

Not Ashamed of the Gospel

Scripture Reading: Romans 1:1-17

Key Verse: Romans 1:16

I am not ashamed of the gospel, because it is the power of God for the salvation of everyone who believes; first for the Jew, then for the Gentile.

Ashamed of the gospel of Christ! Let the skeptic, let the wicked profligate, blush at his deeds of darkness, which will not bear the light, lest they should be made manifest; but never let the Christian blush to own the holy gospel. Where is the philosopher who is ashamed to own the God of Nature? Where is the Jew that is ashamed of Moses? or the Moslem that is ashamed of Mahomet? and shall the Christian, and the Christian minister, be ashamed of Christ? God forbid! No! Let me be ashamed of myself, let me be ashamed of the world, and let me blush at sin; but never, never, let me be ashamed of the gospel of Christ!"[26]

Dr. R. Newton was passionate in his plea of not being ashamed of the gospel. As I reflect upon my life, I have to confess that I have had an easy time of sharing the gospel due to the religious climate in America over the years. Lately, however, I have begun to realize that the religious freedom of the past may not be the same freedom of the future.

In our passage today, we see seven principles about the gospel that Paul is trying to teach the believers in Rome—and to us.

Point 1: We are all set apart for the gospel (verse 1). What an awesome thought that we are set apart! That makes us something special in the sight of God. With this thought, it helps me establish my daily priorities. It's not sports, politics, knowledge, business, or finances, but the gospel that goes to the top of the list.

Point 2: This gospel was promised beforehand through His prophets in the Holy Scripture (verse 2). I must realize that this precious gospel has a historical background that has been documented in the Bible. It's not something that was just recently thought up by a group of men in a dark backroom.

Point 3: We are to share the gospel with our whole heart (verse 9). With a passion and a zeal we are to share this good news with our friends and acquaintances.

Point 4: We are to share this good news with everyone (verses 14-15). Paul says he was obligated and eager to preach the gospel to both the Greeks and non-Greeks, to the wise and to the foolish—to the whole spectrum of life. The message of Jesus can make a difference in anyone's life.

Point 5: We are to take a stand for the gospel (verse 16). Paul very powerfully states, "I am not ashamed of the gospel." Oh, do we ever need individuals and families who can stand together and exhibit a lifestyle that reflects the love of Christ. We need to show the world that we aren't ashamed of this gospel.

Point 6: We need to see the power of the gospel for salvation (verse 16). This gospel is a change agent, giving people real purpose and meaning to life, helping us struggle against the power of sin. Each of us not only knows of this miracle in our own lives, but also in the testimonies of those around us.

Point 7: We are to live a life of righteousness by faith (verse 17). In studying the gospel, the righteousness of God is revealed to us, so we can go out and live a righteous life by the power of the Holy Spirit.

May today's study help us focus on the eternal values of life and not only the temporal. There are a lot of good things to use up our energies and passions, but are they the best priorities for our time and energy? One of our Barnes mottos is: "Say 'No' to good things and save our 'Yeses' for the best." Know what's important and act on it.

Thoughts for Action

❧ Read a good biography of one of the great pillars of the church who reflects the power of the gospel in his or her life.

❧ Share the "good news" with someone you have been hesitant to do so because of various reasons.

❧ Evaluate your love for the Lord. How might you be more focused on sharing the gospel? Write this down in your journal.

❧ Pray to God, thanking Him for sending Jesus Christ to fulfill the prophecies of the Old Testament.

❧ Thank God for your own salvation.

Additional Scripture Reading

1 Corinthians 15:1-6   Luke 24:27-32
Hebrews 11:1

❑ ❑ ❑

Declare God's Power and Might

Scripture Reading: Psalm 71:14-18

Key Verse: Psalm 71:18

Even when I am old and gray, do not forsake me, O God, till I declare your power to the next generation, your might to all who are to come.

As I get older, I think more and more about what comes next. I know there's got to be something else after this life is over, because I can't grasp the alternative. I can't imagine that through all eternity I'll never see anyone I love again, that my whole awareness will just be obliterated. I can't believe that we're only bodies passing through.

...I've always marveled at how belief in the hereafter gets accentuated as people grow older. Until their deathbeds, many of the great minds in science thought that because their soul and being were wrapped up in their body-the old ninety-eight cents' worth of chemicals—and that because after death these would no longer be a body, that was it. But now when they have to go, suddenly they want to believe in somebody up there because they don't know where they're going and they are scared.[27]

There is a season of life which challenges our belief of the hereafter. What happens when we die? The psalmist pleads for

God not to forsake him until he declares the power of God to the next generation. Wow! What a great prayer. I guess that's why I do what I do. I want to tell everyone, starting with my immediate family and branching out to others, about the power and the might of God.

> Lord, I have so much to tell. Just continue to give me a message, give me a passion for the message, give me power to tell the message, and give me an audience who wants to hear the message.

One of my favorite passages that gives me a vision for that all-important message is found in Titus 2:3-6: "Likewise, teach the older women to be reverent in the way they live, not to be slanderers or addicted to much wine, but to teach what is good. Then they can train the younger women to love their husbands and children, to be self-controlled and pure, to be busy at home, to be kind, and to be subject to their husbands, so that no one will malign the word of God."

If only we could grasp the vastness of these words. And some say that being a wife and homemaker isn't exciting and challenging!

Don't wait until you are old and gray-haired. Begin today to share the message of Jesus Christ with the whole world.

Perhaps you're unsure of the message. Read this chain of Scripture to gain God's revelations for salvation.

- Romans 3:23
- Luke 18:13

- Romans 6:23
- Luke 23:43

- Acts 16:30-31
- John 10:28

- Ephesians 2:8-9
- John 14:2-3

- Romans 10:9-10

You can receive Christ right now by faith through prayer.

Lord Jesus,

I need You. Thank You for dying on the cross for my sins. I open the door of my life and receive You as my Savior and Lord. Thank You for forgiving my sins and giving me eternal life. Take control of the throne of my life. Make me the kind of person You want me to be. [28]

If you prayed this prayer, read the following Scriptures for your assurance.

- Revelation 3:20
- 1 John 5:11-13
- Hebrews 13:5
- John 14:21

Thoughts for Action

❧ If you have never prayed a prayer of salvation before and you want to now, kneel before God and repeat these simple words of acceptance.

❧ Read the Scriptures listed which support your decision.

❧ Write in the front page of your Bible today's date. Never doubt the decision you made.

❧ If you have already made this decision for your life, choose a message to be shared with the world. Develop it by starting with your own life and your own family. Then when you have lived it, share it with others.

Additional Scripture Reading

Read the Scriptures mentioned in today's devotion.

Becoming New, Becoming Strong

Scripture Reading: 2 Corinthians 5:15-18

Key Verse: 2 Corinthians 5:17
> Therefore, if anyone is in Christ, he is a new creation; the old has gone, the new has come!

Becoming a woman of God begins with making a personal commitment to Jesus Christ. Only He can give us the strength to change. Only He can give us the fresh start that allows the spirit of godliness to grow strong in us.

Second Corinthians 5:17 reminds us, "If anyone is in Christ, he is a new creation; the old has gone, the new has come!" That's what I discovered many years ago when I, a 16-year-old Jewish girl, received Christ into my heart. My life began to change from that moment on, and the years since then have been an exciting adventure.

It hasn't always been easy. I've had to give up much bitterness, anger, fear, hatred, and resentment. Many times I've had to back up and start over, asking God to take control of my life and show me His way to live. But as I learned to follow Him, God has guided me through times of pain and joy, struggle and growth. And how rewarding it has been to see the spirit of godliness take root and grow in my life! I give thanks and praise for all His goodness to me over the years.

I'm not finished yet—far from it. Growing in godliness is a lifelong process. And although God is the one who makes it possible, He requires my cooperation. If I want the spirit of godliness to shine in my life and in my home, I must be willing to change what God wants me to change and learn what He wants to teach me. How? Here are some of the ways I've learned to keep myself open to the spirit of godliness.

God's Word is the foundation of my security and strength. Only through daily prayer and meditation can I tap into God's strength and love and get a handle on what He wants for my life.

Because I sometimes need a nudge to keep these disciplines regular and meaningful, I have gotten in the habit of keeping a prayer basket close at hand. This pretty little carryall (I like to use a soft, heart-shaped basket in pastel colors) keeps in one place the tools I need to keep in regular touch with God. My prayer basket contains:

1. A *Bible* to prepare my mind and heart to communicate with God.

2. A *daily devotional* or other inspirational reading.

3. My *prayer notebook* (more on this later).

4. A *bunch of silk flowers* to remind me of the beauty and fragrance of the Lord Jesus Himself.

5. A *small box of tissues* for the days I cry in joy or pain.

6. A *pen* for journaling my prayers and writing notes.

7. A few *pretty postcards or notes* for when I feel moved to communicate God's love to someone I'm praying for.

Seeing my basket waiting for me is a wonderful invitation to times of prayer, and a reminder when I haven't taken the time to pray. And it is so convenient to pick up and take to my prayer closet for a quiet time of communion with my heavenly Father.

Where is my closet? It may be a different place every day. (That's the beauty of the portable prayer basket.) Sometimes I settle down at my desk for a quiet time with God. Other times I use the bed, the breakfast room table, the bathtub, a chair by the fireplace, the front yard by the pond, or under a tree—anywhere where I can enjoy privacy.

The actual content of my devotional times varies according to how much time I have available. But generally I start by reading a brief inspirational message from a book. And then I pray. Next I open my Bible and read a chapter or more. (If time is really short, it may be only a verse.)

Next, I turn to my prayer notebook. This is a tool I developed many years ago to help me remember prayer requests and pray more effectively for others. My prayer notebook is a simple 8-1/2" x 11" loose leaf notebook divided into seven sections—one for each day of the week. I've divided all the people and projects I want to pray for—family, friends, church, finances, and so on—into the various sections. For instance, I reserve Mondays to pray for my family, Tuesdays for my church and its servants and activities, Wednesdays for my personal concerns, and so on. (I reserve Sunday for sermon notes and outlines.) Organizing my prayer times in this way keeps me from being overwhelmed while reminding me to be faithful in my prayer life.

I have filled my prayer notebook with photos of people I'm praying for, information about their interests and needs, and special things to remember about them. When I receive prayer requests, I assign them a place in my prayer notebook. I also go through my notebook from time to time and weed out old requests so I don't become overwhelmed. This little book has become a creative, colorful companion that is so close to my heart.

In the back of my prayer notebook, I keep a supply of blank paper for journaling my prayers. This has not been an easy habit for me to develop. I do so much writing for magazine articles, books, letters, and such that writing feels like more work. But for the past few years I have made the effort to write down my praises, my confessions, my thanks, and my requests. I give the Lord my hurts, my pain from the past, my disappointments, and all the questions my mind can think of—in writing. I also write down the convictions of what I hear God saying to me. I'm learning firsthand the benefits of putting my conversations with God in written form:

1. *I am able to verbalize things I've held in my heart but never spoken about.* The act of writing somehow seems to bring up my thoughts, feelings, and desires and to expose them to the light of God's love.

2. *Writing out my confessions helps me get honest with the Lord.* Somehow a confession feels more real when it's down there in black and white. But this means that God's forgiveness feels more real, too.

3. *I can see concrete evidence of my spiritual life*—and my spiritual growth—when I read back over past prayers.

4. *My faith grows as I see God's answers more clearly*— God's "yeses," "nos," and "waits." Writing down the answers I think I hear helps me to discern which ones really are of God.

5. *My obedience is strengthened.* Once again, written promises are harder to ignore than mental ones. Once I have written down my sense of what God wants me to do, I am more likely to follow through.

There is another kind of writing that I often do during my prayer times. Often while I am praying, God will bring to mind someone who needs my love or care. That's what the note cards are for. When God brings someone to mind, I try to stop right there and drop that person a line, assuring him or her of God's love and my prayers. Having the materials right there at hand makes this encouraging habit easy to maintain. It takes 21 days to form a habit. Start today.

Father God, instill in me the desire to commune with You each day in prayer. My days are busy and I often can't get done what I already need to do, but, God, I beg You to touch my life in a marvelous way so I can find time to be with You. Please be near to me and bless me when I'm in Your presence. Amen.

Thoughts for Action

❦ Locate and name your prayer closet.

❦ In your journal write a prayer to God today.

❦ Spend 15 minutes today in your prayer closet. Set your timer. (Make it longer if you want to.)

Additional Scripture Reading

Philippians 4:13   John 11:40
Psalm 55:22   Psalm 37:5-6

□ □ □

Stillness

Scripture Reading: Psalm 46:1-11

Key Verse: Psalm 46:10
> *Be still, and know that I am God; I will be exalted among the nations, I will be exalted in the earth.*

"Be still, and know that I am God," our heavenly Father urges. Easier said than done, right? The complaint I hear from so many women these days is, "I'm just dying for a little peace and quiet—a chance to relax and to think and to pray. And somehow I just can't seem to manage it."

"Stillness" is not a word that many of us even use anymore, let alone experience. Yet women today, perhaps more than at any other time in history, desperately need the spirit of stillness. We are constantly on the move, stretched to our maximum by all the hats we wear, all the balls we juggle, and all the demands our lives bring. In order for the spirit of loveliness to live in us, we must seek out opportunities to rest, plan, regroup, and draw closer to God. And we do that when we deliberately cultivate the spirit of stillness in our homes and in our lives.

As I write these words, Bob and I are at a condo in the California desert. It's July, and the temperature is 109°. But the air is sparkling clear, and a breeze is ruffling the palm tree fronds. As I gaze out over the rippling pool, a deep sense of peace descends upon me.

We've just spent two days of rest, reading, and enjoying each other—letting our conversation roam to cover family, ministry, food, goals, God's love, His Word, and our writing. The conversation has quieted, and I can almost feel my bones relaxing as the spirit of stillness steals over us.

I would say the ideal balance between outward and inward pursuits should be about fifty-fifty. By "outward" I mean working toward goals and deadlines, negotiating needs and privileges, coping with stress, taking care of daily chores, striving toward retirement—getting things done. "Inward" things include tuning in to my spiritual self, talking to God, exploring the sorrows, hopes, and dreams that make up the inner me, and just relaxing in God's eternal presence.

When I was younger, my life was tilted more outward and less inward. As I grow and mature (and perhaps reach another stage of my life), I find I'm leaning more toward the inward. I want my life to be geared more toward heaven. I want to lift my life, my hands, my head, and my body toward God, to spend more time alone with Him—talking, listening, and just being. I want to experience the fragrance of His love and let that love permeate my life, to let the calmness of His spirit replenish the empty well of my heart, which gets depleted in the busyness and rush of the everyday demands and pressures.

I want those things for you, too. That's why I urge you: Do whatever is necessary to nurture the spirit of stillness in your life. Don't let the enemy wear you so thin that you lose your balance and perspective. Regular time for stillness is as important and necessary as sleep, exercise, and nutritional food.

But I know the objection that is already bubbling up in your mind: Who has time?

It's the common complaint—and a valid one.

It's true that the battle is on between Satan and the spirit of stillness. (The father of lies absolutely thrives on chaos and misery!) And it really isn't easy to eliminate all the distractions—the dust, the dirty clothes, the orders that need filling; timers buzzing, phones ringing, children needing us.

Bob and I purposely set aside chunks of our yearly schedule just to be alone with each other and rethink our lives. We work hard all year, fulfilling more than a hundred speaking engagements all over the country. Schedules, interviews, and travel keep us on the move. We have to make space for the spirit of stillness, or we would quickly lose track of each other...and grow out of touch with God.

The door to stillness really is there waiting for any of us to open it and go through, but it won't open by itself. We have to choose to make the spirit of stillness a part of our lives.

I don't mean we need to be monks or hermits. The Scriptures tell us that if we are to live wisely, we must learn to balance the time we spend in quiet and calm with the time we spend in the fray of everyday existence. Ecclesiastes 3:1 says, "There is a time for everything." But that includes a time and a place to cultivate the spirit of stillness in the midst of your busy, productive life.

Thoughts for Action

❦ Read Ecclesiastes 3—yes, the whole chapter. List in your journal from that chapter what time in life it is for you now.

❦ If you find it difficult to develop a habit of quiet time, find a prayer partner with the same problem and hold each other accountable.

Additional Scripture Reading

Isaiah 30:15 Psalm 116:7

Do You Love Me?

Scripture Reading: John 21:15-19

Key Verse: John 21:15b

> *"Simon son of John, do you truly love me more than these?" "Yes, Lord," he said, "you know that I love you." Jesus said, "Feed my lambs."*

Dear Emilie,

Before I share with you a letter I received from my dad, I wanted to give a little background so you would realize just how much it meant to me. A few years ago my parents divorced after nearly 30 years of marriage. (I am the oldest of four children.) Needless to say, so many things changed, particularly my role as a daughter. My life seemed turned upside down. The relationship between my dad and me was strained for a while. Although I never stopped loving him, our relationship would never be the same again. I have done a lot of growing and learning over the years since.

Just before Christmas, I received an unexpected package in the mail. Enclosed in the package was a letter with the following instructions: "Sheri, you wanted one of these a long time ago! Explanation enclosed, read *before* opening." Here is the letter:

Dear Sheri,

You didn't know it but last night you and I shared a *magic* moment together...I stopped at a very small "shoppe" in town to browse. It was pretty cold and breezy, and the owner had a fire going in her potbellied stove in the corner. The room wasn't too well lit and everything was old (well if not old, at least used) and it smelled a little musty...the kind of place you might envision in a movie.

After finding nothing of real interest, I spotted the enclosed item on my way out. I was immediately transported back in time to a similar evening when just you and I went "looking"...(I couldn't afford to buy anything then)...and I *remembered* that wonderful way you had of seeing all the beautiful parts of the world with big, bright eyes and smiles (you were maybe five or six months old). That made me feel as if we were both in a fairy tale...(one nice thing about being older is that you can let a tear fall in public and people seem to understand)! Well, in short, this obviously *belongs to you*...Sorry it took so long! I guess you will always be my bright-eyed baby.

Love, Daddy

Although my dad wasn't aware of all I had been going through with the changes in our family and the confusion I felt, I'm sure he somehow sensed my need for this declaration of love. I will cherish the letter always. (By the way, the gift was a musical "Dickens" box, the kind you shake up and it snows.)

Sheri

No matter how old we become, we seem to always ask this basic question, "Do you love me?" I see it in the market when a child is misbehaving. I see it when a couple is engaged in a nasty shouting match. I see it when a friend is discouraged and depressed at life's turn of events. We all cry out, "Do you love me?"

Many times these irregular behaviors are ways that mankind reaches out and says, "Won't someone reassure me that they love me? I need a touch, a sign, a signal, a hug. Just let me know that I'm loved."

In 1 John 4:7-12 we find another great example of how much God loved us:

> Dear friends, let us love one another, for love comes from God. Everyone who loves has been born of God and knows God. Whoever does not love does not know God, because God is love. This is how God showed his love among us: he sent his one and only Son into the world that we might live through him. This is love: not that we loved God, but that he loved us and sent his Son as an atoning sacrifice for our sins. Dear friends, since God so loved us, we also ought to love one another. No one has ever seen God; but if we love one another, God lives in us and his love is made complete in us.

Let's love so the world can see how much God loves mankind.

> *Father God, put a special message in my heart today to let me know with definite assurance that You love me. Help me to cry out with confidence, "My God loves me so much." May I also realize that there are others around me, my mate, children, relatives, fellow workers, who let me know that I am*

loved. May I also reach out and assure these same
people that they are loved by me. Since You are love,
I want to be love to those around me. Amen.

Thoughts for Action

❦ Go out and feed lambs (real ones and Jesus' lambs).

❦ Write a note to someone who needs a little extra love.

❦ Give a telephone call to someone who needs encouragement.

❦ Does that friend have a special theme for her life (lace,
thimbles, teacup/saucer, gardening)? Send her a little gift
with an uplifting note inside.

Additional Scripture Reading

Matthew 5:44	John 3:16
Matthew 22:39	Ephesians 5:1-2

The Pain of Rejection

Scripture Reading: John 3:16-21

Key Verse: John 3:16a
For God so loved the world that he gave his one and only Son.

Oh, how often we have been rejected in our life! That first date, first marriage proposal, first college entrance application. That first promotion, that first home we didn't qualify for. We have all experienced the hurt and pain of rejection. Let your mind race quickly through that long list of rejections. We often cried. We sometimes called a close friend to let her know of our hurt. Our mom and dad heard our crying out to God, asking, "Why, why, why?"

Jesus faced the pain of rejection even unto death. The people He came to save were the very ones who nailed Him to the cross (John 1:10). Isaiah the prophet stated that the Messiah would be despised and rejected by men (Isaiah 53:3). Even knowing this outcome, Jesus bore the pain of rejection.

On the cross, Jesus shouted to God in heaven, "My God, my God, why have you forsaken me?" (Matthew 27:46). Even His father had rejected Him.

Jesus' life is a reflection of how He met this rejection:

- He never abandoned the mission that God had given to Him.

- He never fought against His tormentors.

- He responded in love.

Paul writes in Hebrews 4:15-16 that Jesus sympathizes with our weakness, that we may receive mercy and grace in our time of need. What a great Savior! He has experienced our pain and can help us.

Scripture has given us some tremendous promises to hang on to during times of rejection:

- "Never will I leave you, never will I forsake you" (Hebrews 13:5).

- "Praise be to God who comforts us in all our troubles, so that we can comfort those in any trouble with the comfort we ourselves have received from God" (2 Corinthians 1:3-4).

- "Having believed, you were marked in Him with a seal, the promised Holy Spirit" (Ephesians 1:13).

It's natural to dwell on the pain of rejection. You can choose bitterness, depression, anger, fear, doubt, or loneliness to dominate your life. But these negative emotions can destroy you. Don't let Satan get a foothold in your Christian growth. There is a better way—God's way. He asks you to forgive and to do good to those who hurt you. He knows these actions aren't just for the benefit of the one who hurt you, but for your benefit as well.

God set the model of forgiveness in Matthew 5:44-45 when He tells us to:

- Love our enemies.

- Pray for those who persecute us.

It's only when we adopt His attitude that we can fully experience His healing of our hurts. If you've been hurt by the poison arrow of rejection, then for your own sake, forgive. This forgiveness prevents even greater pain.

When we respond to rejection with God's love, others will notice the difference. Some will be so moved that they will be drawn to Christ and be saved. God will be glorified, and you will experience the wonderful feeling of spiritual victory. It will not be easy, but it is always worth the effort.

Don't be dragged down to defeat. Let rejection be an opportunity to develop Christian character in your life.

Thoughts for Action

❦ Write in your journal the various remembrances of rejection. Beside each one write the word "Defeat" or "Victory." Praise God for the victories! What could have been done to make your defeats into victories?

❦ If you still have the pain of rejection in your life, go to God in prayer to see what direction He would have you go—maybe a personal visit, maybe a telephone call, maybe a letter. You take the first step.

❦ Be assured of God's love for you during this rejection.

Additional Scripture Reading

Luke 9:54-55   1 Samuel 10:19

❏ ❏ ❏

Humility—God's Characteristic

Scripture Reading: 1 Peter 5:5-11

Key Verse: 1 Peter 5:5b

All of you, clothe yourselves with humility toward one another, because, "God opposes the proud but gives grace to the humble."

As I walk past the Monday Night Football games on television, I see all kinds of strange dances. Most of them occur after a player has scored a touchdown. I can't help but think that a person doing such antics hasn't learned the first step in humility. I was always taught to let your skills do your talking and to act in a calm, reserved fashion. And it's not just football players on Monday night. The world has gone mad with pride.

I believe humility is a foundational character quality at the heart of every successful relationship. Those who exhibit great pride usually don't have strong interpersonal relationships.

Peter writes, "Clothe yourselves with humility toward one another, because 'God opposes the proud, but gives grace to the humble.' Humble yourselves, therefore, under God's mighty hand, that he may lift you up in due time." In present-day management books we read about climbing the corporate ladder, upward mobility, self-assertion, moving on up. It's always *up*. However, God seems to have a different program. The way up with God is always *down*. Peter's exhortation to be "clothed with humility" is a command, not a mere suggestion. God opposes the proud. The moment we allow pride to raise its ugly head, the resistance of God begins.

In Isaiah 2:12 we read, "The Lord detests all the proud." God not only resists and opposes the proud, but He is clear in His teachings that the proud will be humbled. Proverbs 29:23 states, "A man's pride brings him low."

Peter teaches us this truth: When you are clothed with humility, God terminates His resistance against you. As God's children, we should be smart enough to stay on the good side of God by staying on the side of humility.

God always opposes the proud, yet if we are humble, He will exalt us at the proper time.

- "Humility comes before honor" (Proverbs 15:33).

- "Humble yourself before the Lord and He will lift you up" (James 4:10).

- "He has brought down rulers from their thrones, but has lifted up the humble" (Luke 1:52).

Then what is humility?

- It is moral realism, the result of a fresh revelation of God.

- It is esteeming others as better than ourselves.

- It is the fruit of repentance.

- It is the attitude which rejoices in the success of others.

- It is the freedom from having to be right.

- It is the foundation of unity.

- It is the mark of authenticity.

- It is the fruit of brokenness.

- It is the quality which catches the attention of God.

The end result is holiness. Our only response to God's holiness, and that of His Son Jesus, is humility. If you are interested in developing a long-term relationship with both God and others, make humility your goal. As we kneel at the foot of our Lord, He will lift us up.

> *Father God, I want to be humble in all that I say and do. Please make me aware of any false pride in my life. Amen.*

Thoughts for Action

❦ In your journal, list three or four areas of your life which tend to reflect pride. It might be in dress, friendship, business, attitude, talents. Beside each area write what you plan to do to change your attitude.

❦ Why do you think pride ruins relationships? Jot down a few thoughts.

Additional Scripture Reading

Proverbs 22:4   Philippians 2:8
Psalm 45:3-4   1 Peter 2:21

From Clutter
to Contentment

Scripture Reading: Psalm 37:3-7a

Key Verse: Psalm 37:6

He will make your righteousness shine like the dawn,
the justice of your cause like the noonday sun.

James Truslow Adams states, "No form of society can be reasonably stable in which the majority of the people are not fairly content. People cannot be content if they feel that the foundations of their lives are wholly unstable."

> There may be nothing wrong with you,
> The way you live, the work you do,
> But I can very plainly see
> Exactly what is wrong with me.
> It isn't that I'm indolent;
> I work as hard as anyone,
> And yet I get so little done,
> The morning goes, the noon is here,
> Before I know, the night is near,
> And all around me, I regret,
> Are things I haven't finished yet.
> If I could just get organized!

I often times have realized
Not all that matters is the man;
The man must also have a plan.
With you, there may be nothing wrong,
But here's my trouble right along;
I do the things that don't amount
To very much, of no account,
That really seem important though
And let a lot of matters go.
I nibble this, I nibble that,
But never finish what I'm at,
I work as hard as anyone,
And yet, I get so little done,
I'd do so much you'd be surprised,
If I could just get organized!

—Douglas Malloch

Caring for our homes brings a great feeling of accomplishment. Our belongings will last longer and those drop-in visitors will not send us scurrying around to clean up. We'll feel proud to have family and guests arrive anytime.

I have found that when you have a mess organizationally, everything in your physical environment and how it's managed and maintained holds you at your current level of effectiveness. For example, when you're overwhelmed, you can't see anything else. You can't see new opportunities, challenges, or even how to care for another person. You protest, "Are you kidding? I've got too much to handle already."

The messes in the home many times reflect messes in someone's personal life. I honestly believe that if you don't know what you want out of life, it's hard to prioritize the activities of your life. My book *Survival for Busy Women*[29] goes into great detail showing how you can establish lifetime goals and theme verses. Taking the time to establish goals for your life is very basic to helping you clean out the messes that prevent you from doing the things you want to do but don't have time to do.

There are seven basic questions that we need to ask ourselves as we prepare to eliminate the mess and clutter from our lives on our way to contentment.

- Who are you?

- Where are you going?

- What do you need to get there?

- Does this activity, commitment, etc. make you money?

- Does this save you money?

- Does this save you time?

- Does this improve the quality of your life?

These are some very penetrating theological and philosophical questions, but we must answer them before we begin tossing things out of our lives. You might be saying, "I didn't want to get this complicated! I just wanted to get rid of my messes." Believe me, you'll find it nearly impossible to get rid of your messes until you come to grips with who you are first.

The ultimate goal, of course, is contentment. In Philippians 4:11 Paul reminds us to be content in whatever state we find ourselves. One of the by-products of our Western culture is people who are not content with their jobs, husbands, children, churches, homes, clothes, food, freeways, and life in general. We are a society of malcontents just waiting for retirement or the rapture, whichever comes first.

Thomas Fuller says, "Contentment consists not in adding more fuel, but in taking away some fire; not in multiplying of wealth, but in subtracting men's desires."[30] I have a motto: "Less is best." When you don't have something, you don't have to dust it, paint it, repair it, or replace it. When we are young, we strive to consume. As we get older, we try to cut back and eliminate possessions from our lives which rob us of

being content. If we can't find contentment within ourselves, it is useless to seek it elsewhere. It's just not there! You *choose* to be "content" or "discontent." Which will it be? Whichever option you choose will determine if you are ready to eliminate the messes and clutter from your life, home, and work.

As long as you choose "discontent," you will have clutter in your personal affairs. Only when you get right with God and find His plan for your life will you be able to muster up the desire and discipline to make a new *you!*

After you come to grips with who you are and why you are here, you are ready to eliminate some of the time and money robbers from your home. As you evaluate some of these areas, you will be amazed at how this process will change your life. Finding the answer to these basic questions is a lifetime pursuit in growing into the woman God wants you to become.

Develop a battle plan for attacking the various areas of your home. Keep the following points in mind to help you move toward your level of contentment.

A practical and effective motto we follow in our home is "Do the worst first." In many homes that means the garage, the closets, the kitchen cupboards, or just general paper messes.

I adhere to several rules when I'm in the "attack mode" around my house:

- Turn on good, upbeat music.

- No telephone calls.

- No visitors unless you can recruit a friend to help you.

- Have the total family help on the big projects (particularly on children's bedrooms, bathrooms, and garages).

- Concentrate on one project or area at a time.

- Don't attempt to keep everything. Some things have to go (garage sales, church, Salvation Army). Some things must succumb to the trash can.

- No TV or any other distractions.

As you organize, you will find more contentment, and God will be able to make your righteousness shine like the dawn, the justice of your causes like the noonday sun.

With this new-found peace you will be able to take control of your life, and that makes life more meaningful.

Thoughts for Action

❦ Thank God for your blessings of contentment.

❦ List one area of your life in which you aren't content. What can you do to make that a positive statement?

❦ Develop a plan for cleaning up your messes. List in your journal what you plan to do. After each statement, write down a completion date.

Additional Scripture Reading

1 Corinthians 7:17   1 Timothy 6:6
Hebrews 13:5

Thank You, God,
for quiet places
far from life's
crowded ways,
where our hearts
find true contentment
and our souls
fill up with praise.

Hospitality That Cares

Scripture Reading: 1 Peter 4:8-11

Key Verse: 1 Peter 4:9

Offer hospitality to one another without grumbling.

Hospitality is caring. We can entertain all we like, but not until we care does it become hospitality. It doesn't take much—just the heart to care for your guests.

Too many times we feel things have to be perfect: the right time, the right house, the right food. But who says what is right? In my mind a warm, caring attitude makes any time together right.

We have some affluent, fancy friends who have everything "right": silver, china and crystal, candelabras, matching linens and napkins. Inviting Jim and Georgia over to our house is intimidating, to say the least. I can't possibly meet their level of perfection. In my heart I care and love these friends, but my "self" says, "I can't do it. Why am I having them over?"

I was visiting on the phone one day with Georgia and, before I could catch myself, I invited them over for dinner. "Come tonight," I said, "and I hope you don't mind soup and salad." It was a chilly California January day, and I'd put on a pot of homemade chicken vegetable soup. I must say I got excited about being able to have fellowship with such special people. Bob built a fire in the living room fireplace. I threw a checkered cloth over the coffee table, picked what flowers I could find, lit two candles, and served my famous tossed green salad, chicken soup, and crusty bread. We were all on diets, so for dessert we had sliced fruit with a tablespoon of granola on top. Here's Georgia's thank-you note:

> Dear Bob and Em,
>
> I don't know when Jim and I have had a greater evening. It truly was an evening from soup to nuts. The food and sitting on the floor by the fire was a fun change. In fact, Jim wants me to do the same thing next time we have friends over. Thank you for the great idea and a memorable evening.
>
> Love, Georgia

I later heard from mutual friends what a great evening Jim and Georgia had in our home.

Some people complain they don't have enough room. When our children were in high school, we lived in a very small condo for two years. Brad played varsity football, and Jenny was a cheerleader. Bob and I wanted to get acquainted with the young people our children would be involved with, so we suggested having a tostada feed for all 50 football players and cheerleaders after their first game. Our kids thought it was a neat idea. We called it a Mexican Mountain Fiesta.

Jenny and Brad were thrilled and excited to have everyone over. However, we had a couple of obstacles. First, our condo complex had little guest parking. Second, 50 people simply could not fit into our 1300-square-foot-condo—especially 200-plus-pound players and jumpy, giddy, cute cheerleaders. We had perfectly good reasons to say, "Forget the whole idea," but here's what we did. The school bus dropped all the players off at our front door. We converted our two-car garage into a serve-yourself food buffet, set up long tables for the food, and decorated the walls with sheets of butcher paper, pom-poms, and construction-paper footballs. We had each guest sign the paper with his or her name and a cute saying. Many wrote a big, "Thank you!" or "Great fun!" or "Let's do it again next year."

That evening those young people sang school songs and stayed on and on. Bob and I sat in our little family room and the students came in and out to visit with us. We genuinely cared about those kids. One young football player named Scott came in, sat on the floor, and didn't stop talking for almost one hour. He told us things we didn't even want to know, but we just listened. When Scott got up to leave, he shook Bob's hand and said, "Mr. Barnes, this has been a super evening. I don't know when I enjoyed talking to someone as much as I have you." We laughed later because Bob hadn't said more than 20 words to Scott.

Look what we would have missed if we used the excuse that our home was too small! I've found over the years that we *can* do whatever we *care* to do. We still know many of those students, and they continue to remind us of the Mexican Mountain Fiesta.

The Living Bible paraphrases today's passage this way: "Cheerfully share your home with those who need a meal or a place to stay for the night." Hospitality goes beyond friends and neighbors. Invite a visiting missionary or evangelist home for a meal and sleep. Host members of a visiting choir or a work team that's away from home. Whatever the need, reach out and extend your hand of hospitality.

> *Father God, create in me a heart that wants to open my home to others. Remind me not to grumble when I think about having family, friends, or even strangers in my home for rest and food. Let my family have joy in their hearts as we share what You have so abundantly given us. Amen.*

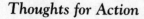

Thoughts for Action

❦ Pick up your phone today and invite a person, couple, or family over for dinner. Set a date on the calendar. (You might even try potlucking and let your guests bring something if they offer.)

❦ Be available to host someone in need from church.

❦ Purchase a good cookbook that emphasizes simple meal preparation.

Additional Scripture Reading

1 Timothy 3:2
Hebrews 13:2

God Has a Plan

Scripture Reading: Genesis 2:20-25

Key Verse: Genesis 2:23

> This is now bone of my bones and flesh of my flesh;
> she shall be called "woman," for she was taken out
> of man.

In his bestselling book *Straight Talk*, Lee Iacocca expresses the importance and priorities of the family:

> My father told me that the best way to teach is by example. He certainly showed me what it took to be a good person and a good citizen. As the old joke has it, "No one ever said on his deathbed, I should have spent more time on my business." Throughout my life, the bottom line I've worried about most was that my kids turn out all right.
>
> The only rock I know that stays steady, the only institution I know that works, is the family. I was brought up to believe in it—and I do. Because I think a civilized world can't remain civilized for long if its foundation is built on anything but the family. A city, state or country can't be any more than the sum of its vital parts—millions of family units....It all starts at home.[31]

In our Scripture reading today we see that God institutes the family. Unfortunately, our secular world is trying its hardest to minimize the family as an institution. We know, however, that God will not abandon what He has begun.

Woman was created for man; she was to be his helper. Man and woman were designed for each other. That was God's plan. Do you have a plan for your family? Have you and your mate taken time to determine what values, what guidelines, what aspirations you have for you and your children?

Marriage causes a man to leave his mother and father, be united with his wife, and become one flesh with her. Is this a description of what happened to you?

Scripture then states, "The man and his wife were both naked, and they felt no shame." Nakedness isn't always physical; it can also include the emotional, spiritual, and psychological aspects of our lives. One of the biggest challenges for Bob and me is to stand before each other "naked" and know that we aren't ashamed. If we've followed God's plans for our family, we can do just that.

If we are to survive as a society, our foundation must be built on healthy families. Let's make it our goal to follow God's plan!

> *Father God, create in me a hunger to search out Your plan for my life. Let me have the wisdom to major on the major and not get sidetracked by the minors. It's easy to get distracted from Your plan, but I so want to follow Your master plan for me. When life is over I want You to say, "Well done, good and faithful servant." Help me today. Amen.*

Thoughts for Action

❧ Meet with your mate and design a master plan for your family.

❧ Write this plan in your journal and write specific goals for each family member.

❧ Begin today to raise good children.

Additional Scripture Reading

Genesis 18:19   Acts 18:8

Femininity

Scripture Reading: Song of Songs 4:1-15

Key Verse: Song of Songs 4:7
All beautiful you are, my darling; there is no flaw in you.

When I was a little girl, I used to dream of being a "lady." The world of *Little Women*, with its gracious manners and old-fashioned, flowing dresses, fascinated me. Softness and lace, tantalizing fragrance and exquisite texture, a nurturing spirit and a love of beauty—these images of femininity shaped my earliest ideas of loveliness.

Is that kind of femininity a lost value today? I don't believe it. The world has changed, and most of us live in simple skirts or business suits or jeans instead of flowing gowns. But I still believe that somewhere in the heart of most of us is a little girl who longs to be a lady.

I also believe that today's world is hungering to be transformed by femininity. What better antidote for an impersonal and violent society than warm, gentle, feminine strength? What better cure for urban sprawl and trashed-out countrysides than a love of beauty and a confidence in one's ability to make things lovely? What better hope for the future than a nurturing mother's heart that is more concerned for the next generation than for its own selfish desires? All these qualities—gentle strength, love of beauty, care and nurturing—are part of femininity.

Being a woman created by God is such a privilege—and the gift of our femininity is something we can give both to ourselves and to the people around us. Just one flower, one candle, can warm up a cold, no-nonsense atmosphere with an aura of "I care." Women have always had the ability to transform an environment, to make it comfortable and inviting. I believe we should rejoice in that ability and make the most of it.

This doesn't mean we have to follow a set pattern or adopt a cookie-cutter style. The specific expressions of femininity vary greatly. When I think "feminine," I usually think of soft colors, lace, and flowers. I love ruffled curtains and flower-sprigged wallpaper, delicate bone china and old-fashioned garden prints. And I feel especially beautiful when I'm dressed up in soft and colorful fabrics.

But I know women with vastly different styles who still exude that special quality I call femininity—women who wear their tailored tweeds or their casual cottons (or their gardening "grubbies") with an air of gentleness and sensitivity. Women who fill their sleek modern kitchens or their utilitarian office cubicles with that unmistakable sense of warmth, caring, and responsiveness. Women who combine self-confidence and an indomitable spirit with a gracious humility and a tender teachability. Women who wear femininity with the grace and confidence with which they wear their favorite elegant scent.

Femininity is so many things. To me, it is objects chosen for their beauty as well as their usefulness...and lovingly cared for. It is people accepted and nurtured, loveliness embraced and shared. More important, femininity is the spirit of care and compassion. In my mind, the most feminine woman is one with an eye and ear for others, and a heart for God.

At its best, our femininity arises naturally, out of who we are, and finds its natural expression in the way we live our lives and make our homes. But in our hectic, hard-driving society, it's easy to lose track of our gentle, feminine side. Femininity is something we must nurture in ourselves and in our homes, and celebrate as God's gift to us.

Femininity can be cultivated in many ways. A fragrant oil or a few drops of perfume in the bathwater. A daisy on your desk. A lace scarf or an embroidered hanky in your pocket. A crocheted shawl around your shoulders. Whatever awakens the calm and gentle spirit within you will nurture the spirit of loveliness in your life.

The expression of femininity is a very personal thing, an expression of a woman's unique self. It is closely tied with identity and with style. Many of the most feminine women I know develop a signature or trademark that marks their distinctiveness. One woman always wears hats. Another enhances her distinctive presence with a favorite fragrance. Still another adopts a theme or motif that becomes part of her identity.

My friend Marilyn Heavilin's theme is roses. All her correspondence is "rosy," whether with a sticker, a rubber stamp, or her own distinctive stationery. Her home, too, is full of roses—on everything from bedspreads to dessert dishes to rose-scented potpourri.

Marita Littauer-Noon, one of my publicists, loves rabbits. When she was little her nickname was "Bunny," and she has carried this trademark into adulthood. Marita and her husband, Chuck, have bunny T-shirts, bunny candle holders, even a ten-year-old live bunny as a pet. Anytime I see anything with a rabbit on it I think of Marita, and at Christmas or on her birthday she always gets a bunny gift. Finding the personalized presents is fun for me and Marita. It's one way of celebrating her unique, feminine personality.

Femininity includes a wholesome sensuality—a rejoicing in the fragrances and textures and sounds of God's world. We honor God and express the spirit of femininity when we get excited.

Look at your body. How unlike a man's it is! The rest of you is different, too—even the structure of your brain. Did you know that women have a higher pain threshold, a keener sense of smell, and better integration between the right and left sides of our brains? I believe we are meant to rejoice in those special feminine qualities that God has gifted us with.

Song of Songs celebrates feminine beauty with wonderful poetry. The woman described there had bouncy, flowing hair (like a flock of goats), sparkling teeth, lips like scarlet ribbons, glowing cheeks, a round and smooth neck, gently swelling breasts, and clothing with the fragrance of Lebanon.

Does that describe me? I hope so. At least, I hope I am taking the trouble to make the best of what God has given me. I may not have time for the 12 months of beauty treatments that transformed a little Jewish girl named Esther into the Queen of Persia. I may never look like a model or a movie star or even my best friend. But I can honor God's gift of my femininity by taking care of the unique me that He has created.

That's one reason I try to be faithful to my exercise program. My daily walks not only help me keep my figure under control, but they restore my energy, lift my spirits, and give me a sense of well-being that makes it easier for me to reach out to others.

That's also why I make the effort to eat healthful foods and prepare them for my family. Shining hair, healthy nails, fresh skin, strong teeth, stress control—all relate directly to the food I put in my body.

And that's why I take that little bit of extra time to pluck and color and brush and cream. A fresh haircut, well-shaped nails, soft lips and hands, pink cheeks, curled eyelashes, pressed and mended clothing—these things help me feel more beautiful, and they tell the world that I care enough to cultivate the spirit of femininity in my life.

And that's why I make the effort to surround myself with beauty. When I do, I myself feel more beautiful. I experience the joy of sharing beauty with those closest to me. And I am motivated to reach out to others with gentleness and care.

Surely that beautiful woman in Song of Songs did that. Solomon speaks often of perfume filling the air, of lush wildflowers and morning breezes. Beauty was all around her, from the wildflowers in Sharon to the lily in the mountain valley.

I imagine that this woman kept fresh flowers around her home, the fragrances permeating the atmosphere. I imagine that she kept the petals and pods from the dried flowers and piled them in a container, adding fragrant oils to make what today we call potpourri. This was sprinkled in her clothing, which perhaps sat stacked neatly in piles. It's hard to say what life was like then—what homes, rooms, furniture, and cooking areas were like. But I'm sure it was simple yet beautiful. I'm sure it nurtured the spirit of femininity in her and helped her extend a spirit of caring to others.

Yet as much as I believe in taking care of myself and my environment, I know that if I put all my energy into self-care I have missed the whole point. The true beauty of femininity comes from within. If that beauty is lacking, no exercise program, eating plan, wardrobe update, or beauty treatment can put it there. No interior decorating scheme can give it to me. Ruffles and perfume are no substitute for inner beauty.

The true spirit of femininity comes from the *heart*, and I nurture it when I pay attention to what is truly important in life. That's why I need the message of 1 Peter 3:3-5:

> Your beauty should not come from outward adornment, such as braided hair and the wearing of gold jewelry and fine clothes. Instead, it should be that of your inner self, the unfading beauty of a gentle and quiet spirit, which is of great worth in God's sight. For this is the way the holy women of the past who put their hope in God used to make themselves beautiful.

> *Father God, You know that my heart's desire is to be a godly woman, one who other women see as a*

reflection of what God describes in Scripture as a beautiful woman. Show me Your way today. Let me be that beautiful fragrance that others want to emulate. Amen.

Thoughts for Action

❦ Write in your journal what makes you feel feminine.

❦ List what you need to do to feel feminine.

❦ Do one of the things you listed above today.

Additional Scripture Reading

1 Peter 3:4   Proverbs 31:30
Psalm 27:4

We Do What We Want to Do

Scripture Reading: Genesis 18:18-19

Key Verse: Genesis 18:19

> For I have chosen him, so that he will direct his children and his household after him to keep the way of the Lord by doing what is right and just, so that the Lord will bring about for Abraham what he has promised him.

———— ❦ ————

My parents spent a lot of time with me, and I wanted my kids to be treated with as much love and care as I got. Well, that's a noble objective. Everyone feels that way. But to translate it into daily life, you really have to work at it.

...Kathi was on the swim team for seven years, and I never missed a meet. Then there were tennis matches. I made all of them. And piano recitals. I made all of them too. I was always afraid that if I missed one, Kathi might finish first or finish last and I would hear about it secondhand and not be there to congratulate—or console—her.

> People used to ask me: "How could somebody as busy as you go to all those swim meets and recitals?" I just put them down on my calendar as if I were seeing a supplier or a dealer that day. I'd write down: "Go to country club. Meet starts at three-thirty, ends four-thirty." And I'd zip out. [32]

We have to make so many choices in each of our twenty-four-hour days. How do we establish what's important? By reconfirming day by day what's of value to us. Our Scripture reading today makes us realize that as children of God we have been chosen and are directed by God to keep the way of the Lord by doing what is right and just. The Lord will bring about for you what He has promised you.

Do you really realize that you have been chosen by God? What a tremendous revelation! We are living in an age of irresponsibility, but as children of God we have responsibility. What are you doing to be directed by God? You can start by always having a teachable spirit. Since you are reading this book, I'm going to guess that you are a learner and want to grow. Each day choose to be a learner and to be directed by God to do what is right and just. We do what we want to do!

Notice that today's key verse points out that the reward for stewardship in the family is that the Lord will bring about what He has promised.

In Proverbs 24:3-4 we learn more about these promises: "By wisdom a house is built, and through understanding it is established; through knowledge its rooms are filled with rare and beautiful treasures." Is the writer of Proverbs talking about furniture, carpets, crystal, vases, paintings? I don't think so. These rare and beautiful treasures are God-fearing, God-respecting children, with good and moral values, children who honor their mother and father and respect others. God has promised these rewards and blessings if only we would abide by His directions. Begin today a new and renewed passion for God's direction in your life.

Father God, let me build my house with wisdom, establish it with understanding, and through knowledge fill its rooms with rare and beautiful treasure. Amen.

Thoughts for Action

❧ Is God giving you specific directions for raising your children? If "yes," what are they?

❧ Write down in your journal what these directions are. Beside each one state what you plan to do to implement these directions.

❧ Share with someone today what one or two of these directions might be.

❧ List a few of the blessings that God has so abundantly given you.

Additional Scripture Reading

Proverbs 27:17   Proverbs 22:6
Proverbs 20:11   Proverbs 19:18

Notes

1. Emilie Barnes, *Things Happen When Women Care* (Eugene, OR: Harvest House Publishers, 1990), pp. 161-62.
2. *6000 Sermon Illustrations*, edited by Elon Foster (Grand Rapids, MI: Baker Book House, 1992), p. 286.
3. Books by Marilyn Willett Heavilin: *Roses in December; Becoming a Woman of Honor; When Your Dreams Die; December's Song; I'm Listening, Lord.*
4. June Masters Bacher, *Quiet Moments for Women* (Eugene, OR: Harvest House Publishers, 1979), March 5 devotion.
5. Lee Iacocca, *Straight Talk* (New York: A Bantam Book, 1988), p. 67.
6. Ed and Carol Neuenschwander, *Two Friends In Love* (Portland, OR: Multnomah Press, 1986), p. 175.
7. James Dobson, *The Strong-Willed Child* (Wheaton, IL: Tyndale House Publishers, 1971), p. 30.
8. James Dobson, *Hide or Seek*, rev. ed. (Old Tappan, NJ: Fleming H. Revell Co., 1979), p. 95.
9. Paula Yates Sugg, *Dallas Morning News*, In Memoriam (September 26, 1993).
10. June Hunt, *Seeing Yourself Through God's Eyes* (Grand Rapids, MI: Zondervan, 1989), p. 33.
11. Robert Fulghum, *All I Really Need to Know I Learned in Kindergarten* (New York: Ballantine Books, 1986), pp. 29-31.
12. Brenda Hunter, *Where Have All the Mothers Gone?* (Grand Rapids, MI: Zondervan, 1982), pp. 108-11.
13. Ibid.
14. Larry Crabb, *The Marriage Builder* (Grand Rapids, MI: Zondervan, 1982), p. 22.
15. Jerry and Barbara Cook, *Choosing to Love* (Ventura, CA: Regal Books, 1982) pp.78-80.
16. H. Norman Wright, *Quiet Times for Couples* (Eugene, OR: Harvest House, 1990), p. 35.
17. Ibid., p. 100.

Notes

---❦---

18. Jerry and Barbara Cook, *Choosing to Love* (Ventura, CA: Regal Books, 1982), pp. 78-80.

19. Alan Loy McGinnis, *The Friendship Factor* (Minneapolis, MN: Augsburg, 1979), p. 23.

20. Robert H. Schuller, *Self-Esteem, The New Reformation* (Waco, TX: Word Publishing, 1982), pp. 17-18.

21. Bob Barnes, *Walking Together in Wisdom* (Eugene, OR: Harvest House Publishers, 2001), pp. 6-7,14,32.

22. Robert Fulghum, *All I Really Need to Know I Learned in Kindergarten* (New York: Ballantine Books, 1986), pp. 17-18.

23. Source unknown.

24. Adapted from Stephen R. Covey, *The Seven Habits of Highly Effective People* (New York: Simon and Schuster, 1989).

25. Jan Congo, *Free to Be God's Woman* (Ventura, CA: Regal Books 1985), adapted from p. 94.

26. Dr. R. Newton, *6000 Sermon Illustrations*, edited by Elon Foster (Grand Rapids, MI: Baker Book House, 1992), p. 309.

27. Lee Iacocca, *Straight Talk* (New York: A Bantam Book, 1988), p. 27.

28. Bill Bright, *Four Spiritual Laws* (San Bernardino, CA: Campus Crusade for Christ, Inc. 1965), p. 10.

29. Emilie Barnes, *Survival for Busy Women* (Eugene, OR: Harvest House Publishers, 1992).

30. Sherwood Wirt and Kristen Beckstrom, *Topical Encyclopedia of Living Quotations* (Minneapolis: Bethany House, 1982), p. 42.

31. Lee Iacocca, *Straight Talk* (New York: A Bantam Book, 1988), p. 17.

32. Ibid., p. 270.